Soldering Made Simple

Easy techniques for the kitchen-table jeweler

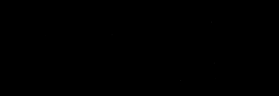

JOE SILVERA

KALMBACH BOOKS

Kalmbach Books

21027 Crossroads Circle

Waukesha, Wisconsin 53186

www.Kalmbach.com/Books

Lettered step-by-step photography by the author. All other photography © 2010 Kalmbach Books.

Please follow appropriate health and safety measures. Some general guidelines are presented in this book, but always read and follow manufacturers' instructions and precautions. Every effort has been made to ensure the accuracy of the information presented; however, the publisher is not responsible for any injuries, losses, or other damages that may result from the use of the information in this book.

Published in 2010

15 14 13 12 11   2 3 4 5 6

Manufactured in the United States of America

Publisher's Cataloging-in-Publication Data

Silvera, Joe.

  Soldering made simple : easy techniques for the kitchen-table jeweler / Joe Silvera.

   p. : col. ill. ; cm.

  ISBN: 978-0-87116-406-3

  1. Solder and soldering–Handbooks, manuals, etc. 2. Jewelry making–Handbooks, manuals, etc. I. Title.

TT212 .S55 2010

739.274

Contents

At its heart, soldering is a simple craft with just a few rules to learn. With practice, the rules will become familiar, the process of soldering will feel quite natural, and soon you'll be soldering custom-made jewelry.

Each step you take through this book will build your skills and your understanding of soldering. Don't expect perfection right away. Allow yourself to make mistakes—they are the key to success. When you take the time to figure out what went wrong and then fix it, you grow in your craft.

It's my goal for you to learn how to solder precious metals (silver and gold, in particular) through the techniques and projects taught in this book. Lots of step-by-step photographs will help teach you how to solder correctly. The language and descriptions are simple. Throughout the book, you'll come across italicized words or terms; if you're unfamiliar with one, turn to the Glossary (p. 109) for a definition.

Part One is a thorough overview of the tools, materials, and soldering and metalworking techniques you'll use. In **Part Two**, you'll learn by doing. The first projects teach you good foundational skills, such as how to solder jump rings and make your own custom findings. Each successive project builds on these skills to teach more about the subtleties of soldering. As you move through the projects, soldering will help you construct some challenging jewelry designs—from hollow beads and boxes to stone settings.

Although I promise that the techniques are easy, they are not watered down. These are the same skills I learned in college, the same skills I practiced during many years working in jewelry shops, and the very same skills that I use to this day. And the equipment is modest: You don't need a fancy torch or a special bench. It's my goal to help you learn how to solder beautiful jewelry at home using simple and affordable tools.

—Joe Silvera

PART ONE
Soldering Basics

In this section, you'll learn what you need for a simple soldering setup—from the easy-to-use butane torch that's at the heart of these techniques to the materials such as solder, flux, and pickle that you'll use in every soldered jewelry project.

I'll also teach you some of the techniques that will help you become a pro with the torch, such as fueling and adjusting your torch and matching your heating pattern to the type of project you're soldering.

What Is Soldering?

The act of soldering is simply joining metal parts together using heat and a fusible alloy that is also called *solder*. (It can sometimes get confusing: The term "solder" is both a noun and a verb.) Soldering is used in the manufacture of almost everything metal related—from munitions to outdoor furniture, electronics to jewelry.

In jewelry soldering, you join metal using heat and pieces of solder. Solder is an *alloy* of metals that melts at a lower temperature than the metal it is joining. Solder is usually composed of the same metal you are trying to join. For example, sterling solder is a mix of *sterling silver* and zinc.

Metal is soldered when you place pieces of solder on a seam brushed with *flux* and heat the metal evenly until the solder melts and flows. When the metal is heated, it expands slightly and creates a vacuumlike draw, also called capillary action, that pulls the melted solder into and through the join. Because solder doesn't fill gaps easily, the two parts to be joined must meet perfectly.

safety warning
Because you may be a "kitchen-table jeweler," remember to keep soldering materials separate from food and food-serving items. Your common sense will guide you, and I also provide specific safety tips along the way. No eating, drinking, or smoking in the area where you are soldering. Clean the space thoroughly after soldering. For more on workspace safety, please see p. 17.

Knowing how to solder will open many doors in your jewelry making. You can use your new skill to permanently close jump rings, attach posts and pin backs, and make custom findings such as clasps, beads, and stone settings. You'll get hands-on practice in making these items (not to mention some charming jewelry) by creating the projects featured in this book.

frequently asked questions

Can I solder jewelry with stained-glass solder?
No. Low-temperature solder, the kind used for stained glass or available at hardware stores, is used for what's called *soft soldering*. It adheres mostly to the surface, forms weak bonds, and contaminates precious metals (and therefore should not be used with silver or gold). High-temperature or jewelry solder flows at high temperatures, on average 1325°F (718°C) and above, and this process is called *hard soldering*. This kind of soldering forms strong bonds that can be bent, formed, and hammered.

What's the difference between soldering and fusing?
Fusing is a way of joining metal by heating it very close to the melting point until the surface collapses slightly, closing the seam. Metals such as *fine silver* and *Argentium sterling silver* fuse easily because they don't oxidize (or blacken) when heated.

Traditional sterling silver, copper, brass, and some alloys of gold don't fuse easily because the copper in them oxidizes, which can prevent fusing from happening. Fusing requires the same high temperature every time a join is made, which is problematic for the multistep joins involved in projects such as stone settings, boxes, and beads—you're more likely to end up with a lump of silver than a piece of jewelry.

Soldering occurs at a temperature that's lower than the melting point of jewelry metals, and you can choose solders that melt at different temperatures for the best control and care of your metal—especially important for the multistep joins mentioned above. Soldering has a few advantages over fusing: Fusing can cause your metal to shrink and thicken, and it can create unwanted texture. Also, with soldering, you have more choices in the metals you use, and you can even mix disparate metals in one jewelry piece.

Soldering Tools

As a jewelry maker, you have undoubtedly amassed an assortment of pliers, hammers, and so on. This section does not detail those basic tools, but rather specifies the minimum items you need for soldering and making the projects featured in this book. Naturally, there are many "nice to have" tools not listed here, which you may acquire as you become more proficient.

TORCHES

Soldering torches come in many sizes and use various gases, such as propane, acetylene, hydrogen, or butane. These gases are often mixed with oxygen to increase the temperature of the flame produced. Professional-grade torches are expensive ($500–$1,500) and use high-temperature flames for fast soldering or melting large amounts of metal. For the projects in this book, however, you'll use only two sizes of a simple, affordable, handheld torch—what's often referred to as a micro or mini torch and its big brother, a jumbo butane torch. You'll be amazed how much work you can do with these humble tools! What's more, you'll work only with butane gas, which is inexpensive, easy to purchase, and generally safe for home use, unlike some of the other fuels. In fact, the smallest of the micro torches are used by culinary students for making crème brûlée.

I suggest keeping two sizes of torches handy: a small one for detailed work and a large one for fast heating and large jobs. (In the project section, I recommend when you'll need the extra power of the jumbo butane torch.) Use the micro torch for jump rings, wirework, and delicate joins. Use the jumbo torch for big pieces and thick metal—the large flame will cover more surface area and heat the metal more effectively. If you try to use the small torch on a big job, you'll find that the heat dissipates as you move the small flame around the large area, and it will be very difficult to bring the metal up to soldering temperature.

There are several models to choose from. Look for a torch that has easy-to-use controls for regulating the gas and oxygen, as these are elements you will adjust often. Expect to pay $30–$80 for a quality micro or jumbo torch. For better performance and to keep your torch working a long time, use the best quality butane that you can afford.

Two sizes of butane torches: the micro (front) and the jumbo torch

SOLDER BOARDS

Solder boards are designed to take the heat of soldering. They are made from a variety of materials that vary in working temperature. For beginners, I recommend using a 6x6 in. (15x15cm) or larger ceramic soldering board.

(Be sure it's a ceramic board made for soldering—a ceramic tile from the hardware store can't take the direct heat of soldering. Do use a large ceramic tile *under* the solder board to protect your tabletop, however.)

Cold boards such as ceramic and Silquar can take more heat than a Solderite board and can slow soldering down, which is a good thing when you're working on small items that are easy to melt, such as jump rings or wire. Solderite reflects more heat and can amplify the heat of your torch, for better or worse.

Solder boards are cleaner to work on than materials such as charcoal or firebrick. When necessary, clean your solder

From left to right, common solder boards Silquar, Transite, ceramic, and Solderite

board with a towel dampened with water. Don't use chemical cleaners; they'll vaporize in your face while soldering. You can remove baked-on bits with a steel-bristled brush; wear a dust mask while scrubbing.

CHARCOAL, HONEYCOMB, AND FIREBRICK

Compressed charcoal, honeycomb, and firebrick are helpful when you want to amplify the heat from the torch to speed up melting or soldering.

Charcoal creates a reducing atmosphere when heated, which fights oxidation such as *firescale*. Soft charcoal is good for pressing in props or pieces to hold them in place during soldering, but you must quench the charcoal afterward if you don't want it to smolder and burn away. Hard charcoal holds heat, doesn't burn away, and lasts longer, but pieces can't be pressed into it.

Honeycomb is a nice, clean surface, but small parts can easily fall into its holes. Soft firebrick, available from ceramics suppliers, is very reflective of heat. It's easy to push props or pieces into firebrick to hold parts during soldering, but it also has small holes that tend to trap stuff such as solder.

I suggest you start with a hard compressed charcoal block and add honeycomb, firebrick, or soft charcoal as your skills increase. When you want quick melting or soldering, you'll use the charcoal block on top of the solder board.

Clockwise from left: compressed charcoal, honeycomb, and firebrick

Don't use any cleansers on your block. Charcoal and firebrick can be sanded with coarse, 60-grit sandpaper to smooth and clean them. Wear a dust mask and latex gloves, and work outside over a trash can while sanding.

SOLDERING PICKS AND TWEEZERS

Picks and tweezers are used to move solder and hot metal. In picks, you have a choice of steel, tungsten, or titanium. Spend a few dollars more for the titanium pick, because solder won't melt onto it, and it makes picking up and moving solder a lot easier. Don't substitute something that isn't made to withstand the high temperatures of soldering, such as a dental tool or beading awl. Use a real pick with enough length to keep your fingers out of the heat.

Tweezers come in two general groups: locking and nonlocking. Nonlocking tweezers are better for picking up small things, including jump rings and chips of solder. Locking tweezers hold when you release them, which makes them great for holding metal during soldering. You need both kinds. I recommend long tweezers with fiberboard handles that will protect your fingers from the heat. Don't use short, cosmetic tweezers—you'll burn your fingers! Use stainless-steel tweezers, and avoid tweezers that have a painted coating, which will burn when heated.

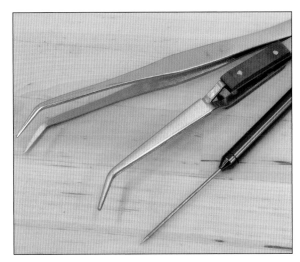

Tweezers, cross-locking tweezers, and a titanium pick

Clean debris and solder from your pick and tweezers with an inexpensive file.

PLIERS

You'll need assorted pliers to open and close jump rings and to shape metal for soldering. Save your expensive beadwork pliers for finishing work and keep an inexpensive set just for metalwork and soldering. (As tempting as it is, don't use pliers to maneuver hot metal, to hold work for fluxing, or to quench your work: You will ruin your tools.) I also suggest using pliers that have one half-round jaw and one that is flat for closing rings and shaping bezels.

A basic set of jewelry pliers: bentnose, chainnose, flat/half-round, roundnose, flush-cutters

TRIPODS

To heat the underside of a jewelry piece during soldering, place it on a square piece of steel mesh over a soldering tripod. The jumbo torch will give you the best results, because you'll need to heat the mesh as well as the metal piece.

A soldering tripod allows you to apply heat from beneath a piece.

THIRD HANDS

A third hand helps you position and hold parts for soldering; it has a weighted base and a jointed holder for tweezers. Avoid third hands that have alligator clips; the jagged teeth are too rough for jewelry metals. Most third hands come with steel tweezers that heat up during soldering. Replace them with cross-locking tweezers that have fiberboard handles, which will protect your fingers from burns.

A third hand with cross-locking tweezers can hold an item in perfect position for soldering.

OTHER JEWELRY-MAKING TOOLS

In addition to the soldering equipment introduced in this section, you'll need many other tools for jewelry making: hammers, files, a rotary tool of some sort, and a few other key items for cutting and shaping metal in preparation for soldering and for finishing into jewelry.

See p. 44 for lists of the basics you'll need at hand to create the projects in Part Two of this book.

Materials

Soldering requires using and understanding a few basic materials and chemicals, including the right metals, flux, a cleaning solution called pickle, and, of course, the right kind of solder.

MELTING METALS

You can melt or solder most **nonferrous** metals or their alloys. Common pure metals for jewelry include fine silver, copper, gold, and platinum. Alloys are made by melting two or more pure metals to make a new metal, such as sterling silver, Argentium, brass, bronze, and karats and colors of gold.

Melting metal allows you to recycle your scrap and transform it into other shapes such as balls to use in your jewelry, as you'll see in several projects in Part Two.

Most plated metals, such as vermeil and copper-core wire, can't be melted or soldered because the high temperatures burn off the plating and expose the core, requiring replating. Bimetals, such as *gold-filled*, are made of two separate metals that are visible to the naked eye. If you cut gold-filled wire, for example, you can see the base metal core when it tarnishes. Melting it will mix the metals into an alloy with a different color. For example, melting gold-filled wire mixes the base metal core with the gold exterior, essentially making the gold disappear. Lastly, avoid melting low-temperature white metals, such as tin, pewter, and antimony, because they contaminate your tools, boards, blocks, and work area.

SOLDERING METALS

Soldering precious metals takes a lot of heat, usually 1200°F (649°C) or more—not as hot as the heat required to melt metal, but still hot enough to burn away any plating or patina. Metals commonly used for jewelry, such as sterling, gold, copper, and gold-filled, can be soldered with various sterling or gold solders, using whichever solder flows at a lower melting point than the metals to be joined.

When soldering gold-filled metal, be careful not to overheat it, or you may create texture or discolor it. The gold layer is very thin and too much filing or polishing can wear it off. Also, when designing with gold-filled metal, keep in mind that any cut or exposed edges will show the base metal inside. Soldering allows you to hide the core, such as when you solder closed a gold-filled jump ring or solder on a border to hide the sheet-metal edges.

11

MELTING METALS	
OK TO MELT	**AVOID MELTING**
Sterling silver	Vermeil
Fine silver	Gold-filled or bimetals
Argentium sterling	Pewter, tin, antimony, etc.
Gold (any karat or color)	Copper core wire
Brass	Craft wire
Copper	Plated metal
Nickel	

SOLDERING METALS	
OK TO SOLDER	**AVOID SOLDERING**
Sterling silver	Vermeil
Fine silver	Pewter, tin, antimony, etc.
Argentium sterling	Copper core wire
Gold (any karat or color)	Craft wire
Gold-filled or bimetals	Plated metal
Brass	
Copper	
Nickel	

Solder

Solder is an alloy that is melted to join two or more pieces of metal. Hard soldering (also known as high-temperature or precious-metal soldering) uses high-temperature solders made from sterling silver or gold. These solders are alloyed with other metals so that they will melt at a lower temperature than the metals being joined, allowing them to blend in and form strong bonds that are durable enough to be hammered, formed, and worn as jewelry.

KINDS OF SOLDER

To make sterling solder, zinc is added to sterling silver in varying amounts to create different grades of solder with different flow (melting) points, including extra-easy, easy, medium, and hard. The term "easy" is synonymous with "low" or "soft." "Hard" is the same as "high" in jewelry jargon. For example, medium sterling solder is 70% sterling silver and 30% zinc. The more zinc in the solder, the lower its melting point. Easy sterling solder has only 65% silver in its content and thus melts more easily than medium or hard solder.

When buying gold solder, you must specify the *karat* and color of the gold. Common karats used in the United States include 10, 12, 14, and 18k (for karat). Gold comes in lots of colors, including yellow, pink, green, and white. Buy gold solder from the same source as your metal for the best color match and specify the color of the gold you are using.

To order solder, specify the metal (sterling or gold) and the flow point. For example, you can ask for sterling easy solder or 12k yellow-gold medium solder. Prices of sterling silver and gold solders vary with the precious metals market.

You'll usually use sterling solder to solder base metals such as copper or brass or when mixing metals. For gold-filled metal, you can use a specially tinted yellow sterling solder. Argentium sterling silver (a tarnish-resistant silver alloy) can be soldered with either Argentium sterling solder or with easy or medium sterling solder. Since Argentium melts at a lower temperature than traditional sterling silver, it melts before hard sterling solder.

Important: If you mix metals, remember that the solder must have a lower melting point than any of the metals being joined.

FORMS OF SOLDER

Solder comes in different forms: wire, sheet, and paste. Every jeweler has a preferred form of solder, and I prefer wire for sterling solder and sheet for gold. Wire solder is easy to cut into different size chips, from small to large, and it can be hammered to make flat pieces, too. Sheet solder is thin and is cut with shears to make small square chips. It's a little harder to make small chips from sheet solder, but it's fantastic for sorting the different karats, flow points, and colors of gold solder, because the type of solder is stamped on the metal. Paste solder has the advantage of being mixed with flux, but it can be too sloppy to be useful for fine jewelry work.

Sheet solder has a stamp that signifies material, color, and flow point.

PROPERTIES OF JEWELRY SOLDER			
STERLING SOLDER	SILVER CONTENT	FLOW POINT	COLOR OF METAL WHEN SOLDER WILL FLOW
Extra Easy	56% (560)	1207°F (653°C)	Light pink
Easy	65% (650)	1325°F (718°C)	Light pink
Medium	70% (700)	1360°F (738°C)	Light red
Hard	75% (750)	1450°F (788°C)	Red

MARK YOUR SOLDER

Whether you buy wire, sheet, or paste solder, it's very important to label it. It's almost impossible to tell sterling wire from sterling solder, let alone whether solder wire is easy, medium, or hard. When solder gets mixed up, mistakes happen. You might accidentally make jump rings out of solder wire, and the rings will melt when you go to solder them closed. Or you might be frustrated that your solder won't flow, only to realize that it's actually a piece of sterling silver wire, not solder wire.

To identify solder wire, I like to bend one end of the wire to create an initial that stands for the flow point: S for soft/easy, M for medium, and H for hard. Sheet solder is stamped with abbreviations to identify it. The stamp usually is in this order: metal or karat, color, and flow point. For example, 18KYM represents 18k yellow medium solder. SE or SSE is sterling (silver) easy solder. As long as you don't cut off the part with the stamp, you'll always be able to identify your solder. Or, if you like to create your solder chips in advance, put them in separate, labeled containers.

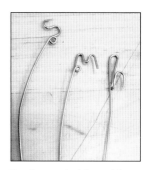

Bend an end of the solder wire to create an initial that stands for the flow point.

frequently asked questions

Why use solders with different flow points?

Imagine you were trying to make a hollow box. You would have to solder together the walls of the box, then solder on a top and bottom. If you used one type of solder for all of those joins, there's a good chance that some of them would melt and open up when you add another side. If you use a higher-temperature solder, such as medium, to solder the first few joins and then use an easy solder for the remaining joins, the first seams will be safe.

For simple jewelry designs, you can get by with using the same grade of solder for several joins. Every time solder flows, it loses a bit of its alloy metal (for instance, the zinc in sterling solder), which is enough to make it melt at a slightly higher temperature than a fresh piece of the same solder.

What's the difference between easy and soft solder?

The jargon can be confusing. Easy sterling solder is sometimes referred to as soft. Because the word "soft" is also used to refer to the type of soldering used for stained glass, electronics, and pipes, I prefer to use the term "easy" when I'm talking about jewelry solder.

What's the difference between silver solder and sterling solder?

Sterling solder is made of silver, copper, and zinc; it is not the same as the silver-colored solder you can buy at a hardware store, which is a low-temperature solder used for plumbing. If you use silver plumbing solder for your jewelry, it will contaminate the metal, discoloring and pitting it. Most of the supplies (flux, for example) used for low-temp soldering don't work for soldering precious metals. Buy your metal, solder, flux, and other supplies from a jewelry supplier or bead shop to be sure you're getting the right stuff.

13

Flux

Flux helps solder flow and minimizes firescale or oxidation. Flux also helps you gauge the temperature of the metal, helps solder stick in place and pieces to stay in position, and changes color when it starts to break down.

Paste flux is a mix of water and borax. A good consistency is a thin batter with no lumps; if yours seems too thick, add a bit of water so it is easy to apply to metal with a small brush. Flux dries out quickly, so keep the lid closed tightly when storing.

At a minimum, apply flux to solder chips and the metal around the join. For metals prone to firescale, such as sterling silver, I recommend fluxing the entire surface of the metal: outside, inside, back, front, and so on. Any exposed metal will blacken with firescale, which can prevent solder from flowing and has to be polished away with a lot of labor. It's easy to protect the metal by applying a little extra flux.

Hard-soldering fluxes turn clear at 1100°F (593°C), just below the *annealing* point of many metals and the flow point of easy solder. As the flux turns clear, it tells you how evenly you are heating the metal; if one portion is clear but another is pasty white, you haven't heated the metal evenly. When flux turns into a clear glaze, it becomes sticky, which is perfect for tacking a piece of solder in place. (Before that point, the flux is likely to dislodge even the most carefully placed solder chips as the water in the flux bubbles and boils away.) If flux is allowed to cool after glazing, it becomes as hard as glass and can glue your pieces to the solder board. In some of the projects, we'll use this trait to hold pieces in position for soldering.

When flux is overheated or saturated with too much firescale, it turns green and then bright blue. This is a signal that the flux is breaking down—the solder may not flow or the metal may be exposed to more firescale. Use this color change as a signal to stop soldering and figure out what is going wrong. For example, you might be applying too much heat or taking too long to heat, both of which can saturate the flux.

Unglazed flux can be rinsed off with water. Glazed flux, which is clear and thus sometimes hard to detect, must be removed with a cleaning solution called *pickle* so it doesn't decompose into a nasty, gooey mess.

You can apply Firescoff with precision if you transfer it to a bottle with a narrow tip. Use a craft paintbrush to apply paste flux.

There are other, more specialized fluxes, including firescale preventatives and retardants, and liquid or self-pickling fluxes. Certain fluxes work better with some metals. A firescale-preventative flux called Firescoff is quite useful, especially for sterling, copper, and brass. In the Koi Fish Pin project, this flux will be used to cut down on polishing time.

Pickle

After soldering, metal will be discolored and covered with baked-on flux. The mildly acidic solution called pickle removes flux and strips metal of some of the firescale that builds up during soldering and annealing.

To make pickle solution, mix granular pickle with water according to the directions on the label. It's best used steaming hot, but don't let it boil. A one-quart electric crock is perfect for keeping pickle warm (dedicate the crock to workshop use only). Hot pickle will clean your metal in a few minutes; if it's cold, it can take 1–2 hours. Pickle won't destroy metal, so you can soak metal for hours or even days.

Traditional pickle solutions, such as sodium bisulfate (sold under the brand name Sparex #2), are aggressive and can put pinholes in your clothing if splashed. Never put steel tweezers into Sparex; the solution will plate copper onto metal. Instead, use copper tongs. Neutralize Sparex with baking soda before disposal.

For home use, I recommend using a nontoxic, citrus-based biodegradable pickle, such as Black Magic Pickle or Silver Prep. These are safer to use than traditional pickles and don't react to steel, which means that it's OK to use steel tweezers with them. Don't combine brands of biodegradable pickle, because mixing them can create a harsh, vinegarlike vapor that is terrible to breathe, especially when heated.

Put the pickle pot inside a shallow glass dish, because spills can damage the bottom of the pot, floors, and tables. Don't reach into pickle with your fingers (even the mild stuff feels like lemon juice in a paper cut!); use long tongs or tweezers. To make it easier to retrieve little parts like jump rings and balls, make a simple sieve by drilling small holes in the bottom of a plastic cup.

A small electric crock dedicated to pickle is perfect for keeping the solution warm.

frequently asked questions

Is flux safe to use?

Flux isn't terribly toxic to use, but it isn't good for you, either. Most flux is labeled as poisonous; borax is used to wash laundry and kill insects. Read and follow the precautions on the label. Use tweezers instead of your hands to handle metal while you flux, and wash your hands before you eat or touch your face. Flux tends to splatter, so wear an apron and keep the area clear of food and utensils. Protect your table with something easy to remove and clean, such as large, ceramic tiles under your solder board. Remove flux from nonmetal surfaces with soap and water.

Can I apply too much flux?

Yes. It will look like the metal is bubbling inside of a pool of clear flux. The solder will float and then flow everywhere but the join. Pickle and start again.

Do I have to add flux if I turn off the torch and stop soldering?

If you can see a clean glaze of flux on your metal, then it's safe to continue soldering. Baked-on, or glazed, flux is unstable, and if you wait too long it will flake off and the metal will need to be fluxed again. If the flux turns bright green or blue and the solder is not flowing, stop and pickle for a better chance of soldering. If you quench or pickle your metal, you have to flux it again.

Should I clean my flux brushes?

Flux is hard to remove unless you stop to clean your brush every time you use it—and if you do, you'll spend more time cleaning than soldering! Use inexpensive craft paintbrushes and throw them away when they're beyond use.

Do I have to pickle every time I solder?

No. As long as the metal looks clean, the join is clear of debris, and the flux hasn't turned green or blue, you can solder again without pickling. Be sure to pickle after the final soldering to remove any remaining flux—otherwise it will turn into a gooey mess.

How do I know when pickle is used up, and how do I dispose of it?

As pickle is used up, it gets saturated with copper and turns green and then blue. Because of the copper content, it's not safe to dump saturated pickle into the water supply, even if it's nontoxic or neutralized. Do the right thing: Pour used pickle into a plastic container, label it, and deliver it to a hazardous waste facility.

QPR After any soldering or melting, remember to
QPR: quench, pickle, and rinse.

Quench the hot piece by picking it up with tweezers and immersing it in a small dish of water. A quick dip is all that's needed. Hot metal can spray when quenched, and it's better to be sprayed with water than hot pickle! Transfer the work into the pickle pot.

Pickle to clean off the flux and some of the firescale. **Rinse** thoroughly in water after pickling to neutralize the piece before you touch or solder it. It's OK to use your quenching bowl for rinsing, but running water is even better. To prevent rust, dry the metal before working with steel tools such as a block, a hammer, or pliers.

Firescale and Fire Stain

When you heat metal with a torch during soldering or annealing, the process often discolors the metal with oxides. These oxides result from the reaction between oxygen, the heat of soldering, and the metal. Using flux can protect metal from oxides to a certain degree, but they can still form. It's just part of the process, especially when you use metal alloys that contain copper, including sterling silver, copper, and brass.

The oxides that form on the surface are called firescale, and most can be removed with pickle. Deeper oxidation that forms under the surface of the metal, called *fire stain*, is harder to remove. Fire stain presents itself as a cloudy, dark gray, or coppery red discoloration. The pickle solution may cover the fire stain temporarily with a thin coating of clean metal, but the surface will still look cloudy, and scratching or polishing can reveal the fire stain underneath.

The most common way to remove fire stain is with polishing, but first you have to recognize it. In the photo, the light gray/silver area is clean, polished silver and the rest is fire stain. If you miss some fire stain when polishing, it will tarnish more than the rest of the metal, leaving a noticeable pattern. If you plan to add patina, you can leave fire stain in recessed areas (the patina will cover it). Some techniques for removing firescale and fire stain are shown on p. 38.

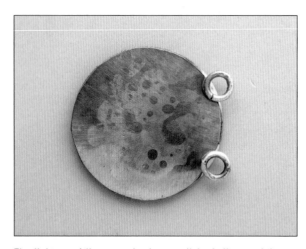

The light gray/silver area is clean, polished silver and the rest is fire stain.

16

Soldering Techniques

With a few precautions and a little practice, you'll be feeling confident and empowered with the torch in your hand. This section takes you through basic torch skills and the soldering techniques you'll use over and over.

Safety First

Read the instructions that come with your equipment and materials and keep them for reference. Keep tools and chemicals away from children, untrained adults, and pets. Keep your work area clean. Material Safety Data Sheets (MSDS) for many chemicals and other materials used in jewelry making are available online or from manufacturers. Another good resource is Charles Lewton-Brain's book *The Jewelry Workshop Safety Report*.

Your best tool for safety is your brain. Use common sense. Stay focused and pay attention to what you're doing. Don't try to talk on the phone, watch TV, or try to manage something else while soldering. Take breaks when you feel fatigued or frustrated. Remember: Your safety and the safety of others are more important than any craft.

PERSONAL SAFETY
- Wear eye protection.
- Remove loose jewelry and tie back hair or loose clothing.
- Wear nonsynthetic fabrics, like cotton, and don't use flammable cosmetics like hair spray. Wear an apron or, if you're sitting, keep a towel on your lap to catch hot metal before it hits your legs or clothing.
- Wash your hands before eating and keep food and kitchen utensils out of the work area.

WORKSHOP SAFETY
- Store fuel canisters away from open flames—especially your torch! Store torches and fuel canisters separately, away from your work area and out of heat or direct sunlight. Butane should not be stored in places that can exceed 100°F (38°C).
- Keep water and a fire extinguisher nearby.
- Keep your work area clear of flammable objects such as paper, plastic, or fabric.
- Allow your torch, boards, tools, and materials to cool completely before storing.

TORCH SAFETY
- If anything goes wrong or you need both hands, turn off the torch. Don't be tempted to rest a lit torch in your torch stand even for a moment—even if it offers hands-free operation. It's too easy to knock a lit torch over.
- Point the flame at the solder board when lighting the torch.
- Assume everything is hot before touching: metal, boards, charcoal, tools, the torch nozzle. Check first for radiant heat.
- Avoid using butane torches continuously for more than an hour without stopping for 5–10 minutes.
- When soldering hollow forms such as beads or boxes, pressure can build and the forms can explode. First create a tiny vent hole to allow pressure to vent. Watch out for water or flux spraying from the vent hole; point it away while soldering, quenching, or pickling.

 safety warning Because the light color of a butane flame is relatively safe, you don't need tinted lenses, but always wear safety glasses to shield your eyes from flying debris. Regular prescription eyeglasses are not enough; consider getting a pair of prescription safety glasses with side shields. You can also have safety glasses made in a magnification (like reading glasses) that will help you see more clearly at a normal working distance. If you graduate to using a more powerful torch, such as acetylene or propane, or frequently melt or fuse metal, use tinted safety glasses made for this purpose. Ultraviolet and infrared radiation from torches and hot, glowing metal can cause headaches or, over time, damage to your eyes.

Work Area Setup

When you set up your tools for soldering, follow these tips to minimize accidents or damage to your table, house, and self. If you use these precautions, you can solder at home—even at your kitchen table!

PROTECT YOUR TABLE

Use a 1x1 ft. (30.5x30.5cm) ceramic tile to protect your table from the torch. Using just a solder board isn't enough, because the heat can pass through it and scorch your table. The tile acts as a buffer to prevent fire or damage from hot tools or metal and from chemicals such as flux or pickle. Don't use the tile for anything else, including heating or forging directly on it. To create a bigger workspace, use four tiles pushed together. Stick-on felt or cork pads will prevent the tiles from scratching your tabletop.

Place the solder board on the tile, right in front of you. Put the charcoal, firebrick, or honeycomb block on the solder board, near the edge opposite you. That leaves space for solder chips and room to solder, too. Charcoal gets very hot. Placing it on the solder board is better than setting it directly on the tile.

ARRANGE TOOLS TO AVOID BURNS

I recommend holding your torch with your nondominant hand (the hand you don't use for writing). It doesn't take a lot of dexterity to aim the torch. You need more control for your solder pick and tweezers. It may seem odd at first, but after a few hours of practice, it will start to feel natural. In fact, a good habit is to always hold a pick or tweezers in your dominant hand; that way you're prepared if you need to adjust something hot while soldering and you're less likely to use your fingers. Reaching across the path of the flame or over the hot board can cause an accident. Place only the torch on your nondominant side. Put everything else you need on the opposite side, including flux, brush, pick, tweezers, and water dish.

USE AN ADJUSTABLE CHAIR

Use a chair that can adjust in height to raise or lower your seat for the job at hand. The most ergonomic position is to sit at a height that allows your forearms to be parallel to the tabletop.

I keep my torch on the left; everything else I need to reach for during soldering is on the right.

PROTECT THE FLOOR

Hot metal or tools can fall to the floor and melt into carpet or burn hardwood. Unless you're working over a surface that you don't care about or that is flameproof, such as concrete, protect the floor.

LIGHTING AND MAGNIFICATION

If you can't see, you can't solder well. Keep an inexpensive lamp nearby, but not directly over your solder board—the heat can melt the lamp or break the bulb. Turn off the light when you want to see the color of heat on the metal more clearly. If you find it hard to see joins or solder chips without leaning in too close to the heat, use headband magnifiers or reading glasses. Depending on your vision, low-power (.75–1.5X) magnification usually will boost clarity and allow you to focus on your work from a comfortable distance of about 18 in. (46 cm).

VENTILATION

Many chemicals used in crafting create fumes. Obviously, if you solder infrequently, the health risk from breathing fumes and chemicals is lower than if you solder constantly. Throughout this book I recommend nontoxic or less-toxic products wherever possible. Full-time jewelers often install an exhaust fan over their solder station. Don't set up in a small, unventilated space like a walk-in closet. A good space is an open area near a window or door that you can open for air flow. You can use a fan to exhaust fumes away from you or out the window. If you find that you're soldering on a regular basis, consider investing in an exhaust fan and hood.

How to Fuel Your Torch

Butane canisters are available in several sizes at hardware stores, home improvement stores, and convenience stores. You can also find small canisters at specialty stores catering to cooks or cigar smokers. Match the size of the nozzle on the canister to the nipple on your torch; they have to seal tightly.

Most butane torches are sold empty, so you'll need to buy butane and fuel yours to begin using it. It's a good idea to read and follow the torch manufacturer's instructions, although you'll find that most torches can be filled in a way that's similar to my recommended process below.

1. Wear safety glasses.

2. Fuel your torch away from open flames, such as pilot lights or people using other torches. If refueling outside, stand with any wind at your back so it blows fumes away.

3. Make sure the torch is off and the flame is out. Turn the gas control off or all the way toward the minus sign.

4. Locate the recessed nipple in the bottom of the torch (remove the stand, if necessary).

5. Shake the gas canister a few times to warm the fuel up.

6. With your arms out in front of you, away from your face, hold the torch upside down, fit the fuel nozzle to the nipple, and align the fuel canister and torch straight up and down.

7. Press down hard with the canister to make a tight seal and to start fueling. If you don't press hard enough, if the nozzle is misaligned, or when the torch is full, the butane will spray back right away. Normally, if the torch is all or partially empty, the butane will hiss into the torch quietly, creating a slight haze in the air. This can take 10–30 seconds.

8. As soon as the torch is full, wet butane will spray into the air. Stop fueling immediately so you don't overfill the torch. If you do, butane will spit out of the bottom or top. Don't use the torch until the spitting stops.

Press down hard with the canister to make a tight seal and begin fueling.

9. Turn the torch upright and wait 5–10 minutes before you use it to settle any air bubbles.

Although butane evaporates quickly at room temperature, it's good practice to wipe off your torch and hands. Keep your torch upright as much as possible; don't lay it on its side or place it upside down. Air bubbles can form in the butane, and they will cause your flame to sputter, go out, or flash a large yellow flame. Your torch isn't broken! Just allow it to settle for a little longer, tap the bottom while the torch is off, or ignite and run the torch in a safe place until the flame is normal again.

A torch could burn for about 20 minutes of constant use, but practically speaking, a refueling will last for hours because each soldering session lasts only several minutes. Normally, the flame from a micro butane torch is a few inches long when the torch is fully fueled. When the flame starts to shrink and won't increase no matter how much you turn up the gas, it's time to refuel.

Wait 5–10 minutes for the torch to cool before refueling. If the flame is short and weak right after refueling, you may have had a problem with refueling. Review the steps above; you may have to try again. To minimize risks, don't refuel your torch before storing it; fill it only at the start of a work session.

How to Light Your Torch

Although you can buy a variety of butane torches made by different manufacturers, many have similar systems for igniting and controlling the flame. Read and follow the instructions that came with your torch. Replace your torch if you suspect a leak or that the torch is broken—for example, you have a weak flame, yet the gas lever is set to "+" and the torch is properly fueled. Light your torch away from flammable materials such as paper, butane, draperies, yourself, and other people. Always point it toward your solder board, which can take the heat.

BUTANE MICRO TORCH

1. Turn the fuel switch all the way to plus (+) or maximum. Press your thumb against the safety switch under the trigger, and pull it down until it clicks and stays in position.

2. Push hard on the trigger. The flame should ignite when the trigger clicks; keep holding the trigger down. If the flame doesn't light, the safety will re-engage; repeat steps 1 and 2.

3. While holding the trigger, hold down the "continuous" button and then release the trigger. Release the continuous button to keep the torch lit without holding the trigger.

4. To turn off the torch, push the trigger again.

JUMBO BUTANE TORCH

   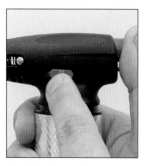

1. Turn the gas lever down until it is just a little above minus (-), or low, on the dial to avoid lighting the torch with too large a flame.

2. Depress the red safety switch under the trigger until it stays in the off position, pointing downward.

3. Push hard on the trigger. The torch will ignite when the trigger pops with a clicking sound; continue to hold. If it doesn't light, repeat steps 1–3 and try increasing the gas.

4. Slide the locking switch toward the back and release the trigger. You can adjust the gas lever to create the size of flame you want. Slide the locking switch forward to turn off the torch. The trigger is disabled while the lock is on.

Adjusting the Flame

Using the right type of flame will help you get the results you want when you're soldering or melting metal. Many micro torches that are sold for jewelry work have an adjustable sleeve that allows you to customize the mix of oxygen and fuel to make the flame hotter or cooler. More oxygen, and the flame is hotter. Less oxygen, and the flame is cooler and more gentle. Fine-tuning the adjustment will help stabilize your flame and keep it from sputtering. Inexpensive butane torches, particularly those made for cooking, may not have such controls and will create an oxidizing flame by default.

OXIDIZING FLAME—WIDE OPEN

Adjust the nozzle until the hole is fully open. You'll hear a loud air flow and see a sharply pointed cone inside the translucent flame. This oxygen-rich flame is the hottest type of flame and will heat your metal quickly. Some butane torches produce only this oxidizing flame. It's good for melting metal and precise, fast heating, although it can oxidize metal and create firescale.

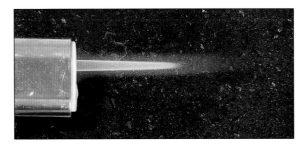
The oxidizing flame has a sharply pointed cone.

NEUTRAL FLAME—HALF OPEN

A neutral flame has a balanced mix of oxygen and gas; it's a hot flame that's less prone to producing firescale than the oxidizing flame. It's quieter than the oxidizing flame, and it has the outline of a cone with a feathered tip. This is a good flame for most soldering jobs.

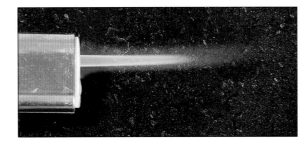
The neutral flame has a slightly feathered tip.

REDUCING FLAME—ALMOST CLOSED

The reducing flame (sometimes called a bushy flame) is rich in gas and minimizes firescale by reducing the oxygen as it heats the metal. A reducing flame from a butane torch is too cool for most soldering or melting. If you use this flame with a charcoal block, which also reduces oxygen when heated, you can anneal, or soften, your metal.

The reducing flame can be used for annealing.

Torch Practice

Practice makes most things better, and soldering or melting metal is no exception. Read through these steps first. The exercises will help you learn how to heat effectively with the torch and how to hold heat at lower temperatures without melting your jewelry.

Part of controlling the torch is recognizing the color of heat on the surface, which moves from pale pink to light red to red to orange. These colors are signs of when different grades of solder flows, when metal is annealed, and warning signs that metal is in danger of melting. The light color of some metals (silver, for example) make it difficult to read the color of heat, especially in brightly lit rooms; try dimming the lights.

1. Turn on the torch, pointing it only at your safe area: the solder board or charcoal block. Adjust the nozzle to an oxidizing flame.

2. Point the torch at the block and keep the flame on one spot until it glows a bright red. The tip of the blue cone inside the translucent flame (the hottest part) should be just above the charcoal, almost touching it.

3. Push farther into the flame, so that the cone is touching the block. You'll hear more air rushing, and you may also see a black, cool spot inside the bright orange heat. This is caused by air blowing on the surface, and it can cool your work, slowing down the melting or soldering process. It's tempting to think that this will help you solder, but avoid pushing into the air cone: It can prevent the solder from getting hot enough to flow.

4. Pull back and continue to raise the torch slowly, keeping the flame pointed at the hot spot on the charcoal. Make a mental note of how far back the torch is from the surface when the spot fades to black. Turn off the torch. Although the heat is no longer visible, the surface is still hot enough to burn you and to melt plastic or ignite paper. The point here is that the heat from your torch reaches a long distance, up to a foot (30cm) or more. Keep it pointed at the solder board or charcoal. Be careful when working with the flame pointing away from the solder board, such as when you're making head pins. Things like nearby water bottles and paper can melt or catch fire. Keep your fuel canisters and other torches at a safe distance from your solder area.

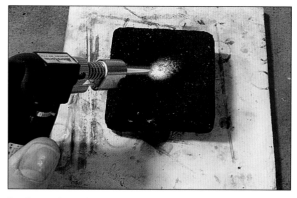

Torch practice will help you learn how to position the flame for maximum effectiveness and simmer the heat at lower temperatures without melting your jewelry.

5. Turn on the torch and point it at the charcoal block, creating a bright orange spot of heat. Bring the tip of the blue cone down so that it hovers just above the surface. This is how close you should be for maximum heat when melting, balling up solder, or building up heat for soldering. The longer you stay focused on this spot, the hotter it will get. If you keep your torch too long on the metal, you can melt it or fry the surface, creating unwanted texture.

6. Pull the flame away from the block to lower the heat to a red color. Move the flame in a quick circle above the spot. Notice how the heat dulls or disappears. Moving too quickly like this can prevent your metal from ever getting hot enough to solder or melt. Bring the flame back to the spot and move in a slow circle, spiraling the heat. The block will glow brighter, moving to orange. The slower you move the torch, the faster the heat will build.

7. Steady the torch and focus on the charcoal to make a red spot again. Pull the flame away and move it on and off the spot to simmer the heat without it getting any hotter. Controlling the heat from the torch is critical to soldering. You have to work with the flux and solder at lower temperatures in order to be able to place solder and position pieces to be joined. Too much heat, and solder will flow everywhere, without any control. Simmering the heat in this way extends your working time until you're ready to solder. Turn off the torch.

How to Solder

Most soldering combines the same steps in roughly the same order to get the job done. Practicing these steps will help it all to become more intuitive, so you'll have a better understanding of why soldering works and what to fix when it doesn't.

1. Clean your metal and tools. Dirt, skin oil, tarnish, and grease can stop solder cold and push away flux, exposing metal to firescale. Clean your piece with rubbing alcohol, soap and water, or by pickling it. Rinse it thoroughly. Too much firescale will also prevent solder from flowing; sand the piece with 600-grit paper. Handle the metal with tweezers rather than your fingers as much as possible. Finally, tools such as solder boards, blocks, and picks need to be clean, too. Dirty tools and sticky old flux can make it hard to place solder. Clean any baked-on flux from your pick or tweezers with an old file.

2. Close the join. The join should be as tight as possible. Solder is very good at flowing along a flush seam. It isn't good at filling gaps. Check the join carefully for any gaps and fix them before soldering.

3. Apply an even coat of flux to all surfaces of the jewelry piece. Flux helps solder to flow, minimizes firescale, helps gauge the temperature of the metal, helps solder stick in place and pieces to stay in position, and changes color when it starts to break down.

4. Cut solder and apply flux to it. A little bit of solder goes a long way! Use the minimum amount to fill the join; if you have too much solder, you will have to polish it off later.

5. Clear the flux on the piece. Warm the metal until the flux turns into a clear glaze.

6. Apply the solder to the piece. Solder wants to stick to warm flux and warm metal. Keep the metal warm, but not too hot, while you position the solder with tweezers or a pick. The flux should be clear, and the metal should be matte and clean looking. It should not glow pink or red at all. If the metal is too hot, the solder will flow everywhere as soon as it's applied.

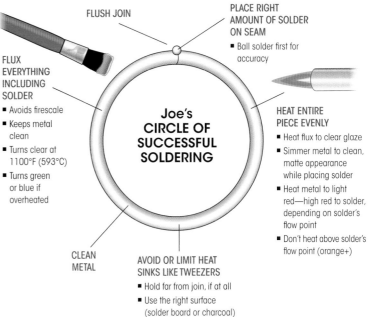

7. Heat evenly. Bring the torch closer and move slowly to increase the heat for soldering. Be sure to evenly heat the entire piece, not just the join. Silver, gold, and copper conduct heat really well, and the heat will be pulled away from the join. Heat the rest of the metal first and then bring the heat to the join. Also, heat the thickest parts more because they will take longer to get to soldering temperature. Solder will flow first to the hottest part—typically the thin, small areas.

8. Watch for solder to flow. You'll see a few indications as the metal gets close to soldering temperature. Look for a light pink or red glow, depending on the flow point of the solder. The flux will get even clearer, and the silver will whiten. You may see a faint green hue in the flux. Suddenly the solder will flow in a molten silver streak into the joins and seams. As soon as it does, remove the heat. Too much heat and the solder will boil, leaving pits in the join.

9. Move it before it sticks. Move the metal before it cools and sticks to the charcoal block or solder board. If it sticks, it's being held by hardened flux. Use a little heat from the torch to loosen the flux and move it with your pick or tweezers. Don't pry it up or you'll take chunks of charcoal or solder board with it!

10. QPR: Quench. Pickle. Rinse. Quench your metal in a small bowl of water before pickling to avoid spraying pickle all over. Pickle for 2–5 minutes for a quick cleaning before continuing to solder. When all soldering is complete, pickle for a longer period, 20 minutes or more, to remove as much firescale as possible. Rinse off the pickle solution in water. Pickle can discolor tools and interfere with soldering.

23

CUTTING SOLDER

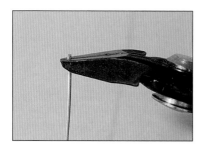

1. Use flush cutters. Place the flat side toward the tip of the solder wire.

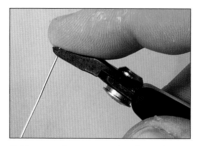

2. Put your finger over the tip before you cut.

3. Catch the solder on your finger and place it on the solder board.

SOLDER CHIP SIZES

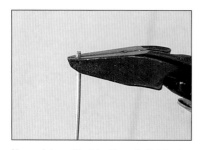

Normal (small) chip (1mm): Cut just below the bevel at the end of the solder wire.

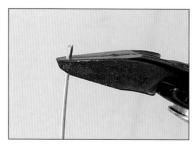

Double length (2–3mm)

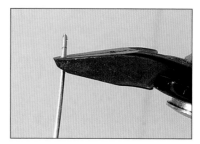

Triple length (3–4mm)

STAGES OF FLUX

As flux is heated, it goes through a few stages before it turns clear, the stage at which it's time to apply solder. It's important not to apply solder too soon, otherwise the flux may bubble and move your solder chips. Gauging the temperature of the metal by the stage of the flux will help you succeed.

1. White powder. Most of the water has boiled off, and the metal is a few hundred degrees Fahrenheit.

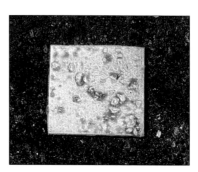

2. Dirty goo. Before it goes clear, the flux will look dirty, gooey, and nasty. Note that bubbles can push solder pieces out of place.

3. Clear. The goo goes clear, revealing the color of the metal, which is around 1100°F (593°C) and ready to accept solder. The sticky flux can hold parts together. If it cools, it will look the same but solder won't stick; warm it again to apply solder.

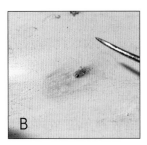
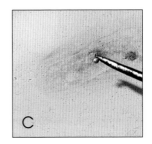
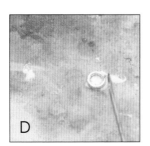

HOW TO PICK-SOLDER

Tweezers are sometimes cumbersome when you need to precisely place solder, and solder may even melt onto them. To place solder with precision, melt a chip into a small ball and scoop it up with a pick. The small footprint of the ball will sit exactly on the smallest seam. Using just enough solder to close a join also means less polishing later. Follow these steps for precision soldering.

1. Clean your pick. Remove any baked-on flux or solder from your pick with an inexpensive file. Support the end of the pick on the edge of your table. File on the forward stroke.

2. Cut and flux the solder. Use flush-cut pliers to cut a small chip of solder. Lightly flux the chip and place it on the charcoal block or solder board **[A]**.

3. Melt the solder. Keep the pick close to but not in the flame. Place the tip of the cone close to the chip. Heat until the chip turns into a ball and glistens as if wet like a ball of mercury **[B]**.

Don't let the ball glow red or orange. That's too hot and it will smear on the board or pick.

4. Scoop with the pick. Move the flame away as you scoop up the solder with the tip of the pick. Turn the pick so that the solder is hanging down **[C]**. The ball should be lightly tacked to the pick and come off easily with a little heat if you roll it against the solder board.

5. Warm the metal. Warm the piece you want to solder until the flux clears and the metal turns a clean, matte color. Hold the metal at this temperature while you touch the solder on the pick to the join **[D]**. (If the solder bounces off, the metal is too cool.) When the metal is warm enough, the ball will slip from the pick to the join. Make sure it's centered on the join line. While the flux is warm, it's tacky, and the solder can be moved around. Don't let the metal get too hot (glowing pink or red).

6. Continue heating. Watch for the solder to flow.

SWEAT-SOLDERING

Sweat-soldering is a two-step method that can be a clean and easy solution for some joins. It's usually used to join two separate parts, such as two pieces of sheet metal, a post to an earring back, or a ball of silver to a base. In sweat-soldering, solder is melted onto one part and spread over the surface like a plating. Then the two parts are put together and heated evenly until the solder flows between them.

Because you can't see the solder, catching the signals that it is flowing can be tricky. Telltale signs are the right color of red around the join for the type of solder used (see chart on p. 12). Solder may seep out around the edges of the adjoining surfaces, and the top piece may drop a bit as it settles.

tip
BEWARE OF PHANTOM SOLDER! If a ball seems to disappear when you try to scoop it or place it, it was just a ball of flux, not solder.

HEAT PATTERNS FOR SOLDERING

Jewelry metals and their alloys conduct heat very well, so it's important to heat them properly. How to aim, increase, hold, and decrease heat is covered on p. 22. Here are some strategies for leading heat to a specific form of metal and how to move the heat around for successful soldering.

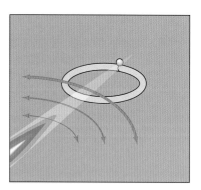

Jump ring: Start with the torch a little farther back. Heat the jump ring from the side opposite the join. After applying solder, direct the flame straight up the middle, through the join.

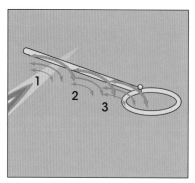

Wire: Start warming the wire farthest away from the join. Shift the heat to the join and then heat forward and back, until the flux clears evenly on all parts. Repeat after applying the solder and then dwell on the join.

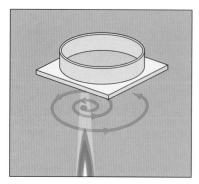

Bezels and boxes: When soldering a bezel or sides of a box to a base, heat from underneath, moving the tip of the cone just below the metal in a slow spiral. if you heat from the top, you may overheat the thin bezel.

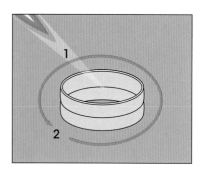

Tall stack: When soldering a stack together (for example, two rings to make a wide band), heat around the outside and then inside. It can be easier to move the heat evenly around the stack if you put your solder setup on a turntable made for soldering.

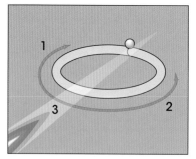

Large ring: The metal opposite the join will pull all the heat away. Start by heating the back of the ring, move up both sides, then dwell on the join. When the flux clears, apply solder. Repeat this pattern, dwelling longer on the join with each repetition.

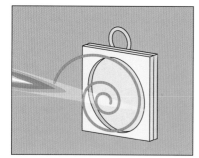

Thick and thin: Focus the heat on the thickest part, away from a thin, small part that you're adding, like a jump ring. Point the flame sideways, away from the thinnest part, and focus the heat over the rest of the metal. Repeat after applying the solder. Watch the solder. If it starts to move toward the thick piece only, swing the heat to the thin part.

TROUBLESHOOTING

PROBLEM	PROBABLE CAUSES	SOLUTIONS
Not enough heat	■ Your torch could be getting low on butane. Refuel it. ■ Try a bigger torch. ■ A heat sink is drawing heat away. ■ The flame is fluttering or incorrect. Adjust your torch.	■ Holding the metal too close to the join with steel tweezers or a third hand will pull heat away. Use the minimum amount of steel and hold as far from the join as possible. ■ Cold surfaces such as solder boards and steel can also be a heat sink for medium to large projects. Switch to a charcoal block, firebrick, or honeycomb block. Use a larger torch. ■ The steel mesh of a soldering tripod requires more heat. Use a larger torch. ■ Metal heats fastest when it has maximum exposure to the torch. Use props such as third hands, firebricks, and charcoal to raise the metal so you can heat it from underneath, too. ■ When all else fails, stop and clean your work in the pickle. Then set it up again, look for mistakes, and try again. Don't try to force the solder to flow by overheating your piece or trying too long—you'll only succeed in melting it or covering it in firescale. Look for the reason why it's not soldering and correct the problem.
Solder flows away from the join	■ The join isn't closed. Stop and close it. ■ Too much heat on one side. Try to heat the metal evenly. ■ Thick and thin areas. Heat the thickest parts more.	
Metal melts before the solder	■ Either you used solder instead of metal to make your jewelry, or the solder you chose melts at a higher temperature than the metal.	
The solder won't flow	■ Double-check that you used solder. You may be using regular silver or gold. ■ Not enough heat (see above). ■ The metal is in a pool of too much flux. Stop and pickle. ■ The solder or join is dirty. Stop and pickle. Sand or file to clean off dirt, firescale, or tarnish.	

UNSOLDERING

Sooner or later, you'll solder something in the wrong place. My favorite is the just slightly askew jump ring that bothers you every time you look at it.

Well, luckily, what can be soldered can be unsoldered! It's basically just like soldering. Flux everything, as usual, and begin heating the metal. When the solder melts and flows again, pull the pieces apart with tweezers or a solder pick. Hold one part down with another tool or wire while you pull the other part off. Use a third hand or tie it to a charcoal block with dark annealed steel binding wire. Afterward, pickle everything and set up for soldering again. Some solder is probably still on the pieces, so you might not have to add more.

Metalworking Techniques

In addition to understanding soldering techniques, you'll need to be skilled in a few other ways of working with metal to complete the projects in this book. Here's a brief course in annealing, filing, drilling, sawing, and other basic metalworking techniques.

Annealing

If your metal becomes work-hardened, you can always anneal it to return it to a dead-soft, malleable state: Simply heat it and quench it. Sterling silver and gold anneal at around 1200°F (649°C), when they glow light red. Brass and copper anneal when they are medium red. Hold the color for one minute, remove the flame, and as soon as the redness disappears, quench the metal in water. Practice will help you gauge the correct color for the metal you anneal.

I recommend using the jumbo butane torch for fast annealing. Follow these steps:

1. Apply flux. Flux protects metal and tells you when it is starting to anneal. Without flux, metals such as sterling, copper, and brass will get lots of firescale when exposed to the high temperatures of annealing. Plus, it can be hard to see the early stages of red heat on light metals like silver. Flux turns clear at 1100°F (593°C), which is very close to the annealing point of sterling. Flux all sides completely. Fill in any gaps while the metal is at a low temperature and the flux is powdery white. For even less firescale, use a preventative flux such as Firescoff.

2. Place on a charcoal block. Charcoal helps keep your metal clean and reduces firescale because it reduces oxygen during heating. The side facing the charcoal will be the least oxidized.

3. Add heat. Dim the light, if possible, to better see the color as you heat the metal evenly with a torch. Another trick for spotting the annealing point is to mark your metal with an ordinary permanent marker such as a Sharpie. The lines will disappear when the metal reaches the annealing temperature.

4. Hold. Back the flame away a little and hold a light red color on the surface for one minute. Don't let the metal get hotter and glow red or orange, or you might melt it or create texture!

5. Quench. Remove the flame and let the metal cool for a few seconds until it turns dark and no longer glows red. Quench it all at once in water. Sterling, brass, and copper are more malleable if quenched after annealing.

6. Pickle. Soak the metal in hot pickle for 5–10 minutes. If the metal was well protected, it should have very little firescale. If it wasn't protected, the surface will be black or blotchy with coppery red patches—oxidation that will require a considerable amount of polishing to remove.

Use the jumbo butane torch for fast annealing.

Hammering

Hammers shape, *forge*, and texture metal. Use ordinary unpolished hammers, such as household ball-peen or claw hammers, to hit steel punches and stamps. You can also use a special hammer for metalwork called a *chasing hammer*, which is made for hitting tools like these. The wide face is flat or slightly curved so that it's easy to hit the end of the punch. Hold the handle at the round, thick end, for easy, repetitive hammering, and use the ball side of the hammer to work directly on metal.

You may already use a polished chasing-style hammer for working directly on wire or metal. Reserve a hammer like this for that purpose to preserve its surfaces; any pattern or defect on the hammer will imprint on soft jewelry metals. Polished hammers have a smooth surface that burnishes and polishes metal; they are also shaped to avoid nicking metal with the edges of the hammer's face. Don't use them to hit tools, such as punches and stamps, which are made of much harder steel. If you do use a polished hammer on steel, you'll ruin the surface, though the hammer can be polished again.

Hammering on metal creates texture. The shape and curve of the hammer face influences the texture, from subtle to obvious. Texture hammers have patterns embossed on their faces for directly stamping metal. When trying to texture both sides of your metal, keep in mind that the texture on the first side will be flattened as you texture the second side. Hammering also forges the metal, making it harder and larger, and possibly distorting the shape.

Follow these steps for hammering your metal pieces:

1. Hold the hammer with a loose but firm grip. Hold the thick grip of the handle with your index finger resting on the narrow neck. Use your index finger as a pivot and squeeze your thumb against the handle to guide the hammer head. Swing the hammer in your hand, allowing your palm to act as the stopping point. A looser grip lets the hammer bounce up after you strike, giving you half the swing for free, and reduces wrist strain. Practice by trying to hit the same spot on a foam mouse pad. For more help with your aim, keep the same loose but firm grip, but point your index finger on top of the handle.

An assortment of hammers with a steel bench block in a rubber base.

2. Place the metal on a steel block. Make sure the block is clean and smooth. Place the block on a cushion, like a mouse pad, to soften the noise. Keep the metal in the middle of the block. The metal moves while you work and can slide away from edges or corners, possibly nicking your hammer.

3. Curl your fingers that hold the metal. Use your other hand to hold the metal flat to the block where you strike and to move it as you hammer. Keep your fingers curled under to avoid smashing them!

4. Flatten with a plastic or rawhide *mallet*. Place the concave side down on the steel block, remove your fingers, and pound the metal flat. Flip it over and repeat to flatten it again. If the metal is hardened and won't flatten easily, anneal it or try tapping it with a hammer with a polished, slightly curved face.

Filing

Filing refines the metal's shape and removes defects such as scratches and excess solder before polishing. Use coarse files to remove metal quickly and fine files to create a smooth finish.

Files come in large sizes for fast work, and smaller versions (called needle files) for detail work. The higher the number, the finer the file. For example, a #4 file is much finer than a #0. Files come in different shapes, such as flat, round, triangular, and half-round. The half-round file is handy for filing almost everything: Use the flat side for straight edges and convex curves, and use the round side for concave curves. A barrette file is tapered on the end and has teeth only on its flat side. The other side has a smooth, triangular safety edge, which makes it good for filing corners. Match other shapes, such as triangular, square, and round, to the shapes you're filing.

Unlike the irregular grit of sandpaper, which allows sanding in any direction, steel files have rows of teeth, so you need to file in the right direction to be effective. File forward: Apply more pressure as you file away from yourself. Filing backward or toward yourself will not remove much metal at all.

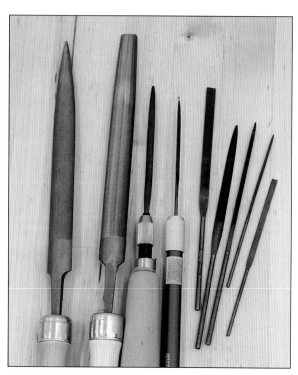

Useful basic files (from left): #4 fine half-round file; #0 medium half-round file; half-round and round needle files in pin vise handles; assorted basic and mini needle files

tip
RECLAIM THAT DUST Try to capture the dust from filing, especially from precious metals such as silver and gold. You can turn in your metal shavings and dust for credit toward new metal. When I'm not at my jewelry bench, which has a built-in collector, I catch the dust in a shallow tray on my lap. Sweep the dust into separate, labeled containers. Save big scraps in labeled containers to melt or to use for other projects. You may be surprised at how much dust and scrap you'll collect after making all the projects in this book!

HOW TO FILE METAL

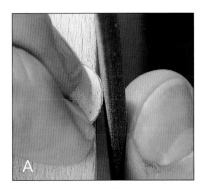

Remove excess metal.

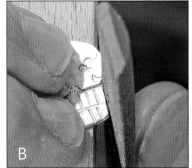

Refine the shape and clean up any defects.

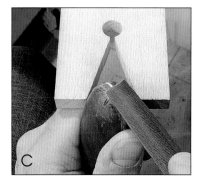

Polish away rough texture on the edges by filing.

Support your work on a bench pin. Use a V-slot *bench pin* clamped to your work surface. Protect your table with a scrap of leather under the pin and a thin piece of wood between the table and the clamp underneath. Sit directly in front of the V-slot of the pin and brace the metal against the wood with your fingers.

File the shape. If you're working with a pattern glued to the metal, file to the outline and remove any excess metal **[A]**. Let the edge you're filing overhang the side of the bench pin a little. Work close to the thick wood edge, which will help you keep the file perpendicular to the edge. Working this way will make a smooth shape, and the top will be a mirror image of the back. If you file at an angle or work without support, the edges will look rough and random, and your piece will get distorted. Filing correctly now means less work later!

File the edges. After the shape is refined, file the edges to remove any high points and rough file marks **[B]**. You can

hold the metal in a *ring clamp* for easier filing: Choose the straight or curved side to match the edge you're filing. Insert the ring clamp wedge on the opposite side and push it in to tighten the clamp. Tap the wedge on your table to tighten it more. If the metal is too thin, angle the wedge a little to push it in further. Brace the clamp in the V-slot of your bench pin while you file. Turn the wedge sideways to open the clamp.

File a straight edge. Hold the piece in a ring clamp and brace it against the bench pin. Use the flat side of a straight file to file evenly across the edge. Start at the tip and file straight or at a slight angle across the edge as you move to the back of the file. To avoid tapering, file 2–3 strokes and then reverse the piece to file from the other direction. Check your work against the straight file for gaps. Rest your index finger on top of the file as you work to feel the angle.

Keep the file flat against the edge of the metal. Look at the edge after each stroke.

It should be flat and not beveled. Try not to hit the corners when you start or finish each file stroke or you could round them over. Land on the edge and lift the file off at the end. Doing this correctly will make the edge straight and smooth. For a really nice finish, file again with a fine #3 or #4 file to remove coarse file marks.

File a curve. Working a curve is slightly different. Use the round side of the ring clamp braced in the V-slot of the bench pin **[C]**. Start with the metal angled away from you. As you file across the edge, rock the clamp back toward you to extend your stroke. If you prefer, you can turn the clamp and angle it away from you, so that you can see the curve of the metal. Rest your index finger on top of the file and work across the edge horizontally. Your focus is on the shape and curve of the metal. But you can't see the edge after each stroke, so check your work often. Open the clamp and change position to file the next section.

Drilling

Use a handheld rotary tool, drill press, or flexible shaft machine (commonly called a flex shaft) to drill holes in your metal. (Rotary tools and flex shafts are described on p. 38.)

Inexpensive, small drill presses make it easier to drill holes because they keep the drill straight for you as you raise and lower the drill with a handle. Use only drill bits rated for metal. Drill a pilot hole (a small hole in the correct position) for holes larger than 1/16 in. (1.6mm). Follow the directions that come with your tool to load and remove your drill bits.

Whichever tool you use, follow these steps when drilling your metal pieces.

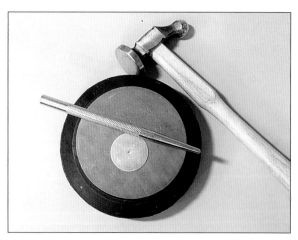

1. Use a center punch. Place the metal on a steel bench block and strike the *center punch* with an unpolished hammer to mark the spot where you want to drill. The impression will keep the drill from skipping around and scratching the metal.

2. Hold the metal with a ring clamp. Metal gets hot during drilling and can catch on a drill bit, pulling it out of your hands and causing injury. Use a ring clamp to protect your fingers.

3. Place the metal on a block of wood. When the drill pierces the metal, it's going to try to enter whatever is underneath—including fingers or a nice kitchen table! A wood scrap is ideal. Don't drill on top of other metals, even a steel block.

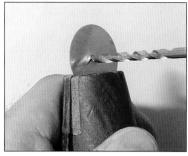

4. Practice placing the drill bit with the motor off. Practice finding the center punch mark and holding the drill perpendicular to the metal.

5. Turn the motor on high speed. Make sure the bit doesn't wobble when you turn on the drill. If it does, stop and reload it. Small drill bits work best at faster speeds. Turn the speed dial up to 10 on a rotary tool or press down more on the foot pedal of the flex shaft. If you're using a flex shaft, wait until step 7 to turn on the motor.

6. Hover over the metal and find the center punch mark. Take your time and keep the drill bit off the surface until you're above the center punch mark.

7. Drill with gentle pressure. Touch the drill bit to the mark, hold the drill straight up and down, and press gently to let it cut through the metal. Don't press too hard or you could snap the drill bit or jam it. However, don't be too light with the pressure either; holding the drill too long on the metal without cutting can overheat and dull the bit, which could cause it to jam.

The drill will want to plunge deep into the wood after you pierce the metal. As it gets close to breaking through the metal, ease the pressure on the drill a little and pull up as soon as the bit hits wood. If the drill bit gets stuck, turn off the motor or reverse it to remove the bit. Rotary tools and some flex shafts don't have a reverse; turn the motor on low speed while you hold the metal firmly with the ring clamp, and try to pull the bit out. If it still won't come out of the metal, take the bit out of the tool and try to twist it out with pliers. If a bit breaks and a little piece is stuck in the hole, use a slender punch to knock it out.

8. Remove burs. Drilling will make sharp burs around the hole. Dull bits and soft metals such as copper create more burs. Use a sharp, unused drill bit to remove the burs. A ⅛-in. (3.2 mm) or ¼-in. (6.4 mm) drill bit works great for this job; just turn the bit gently around the inside of the hole. Don't press too hard and don't angle the bit as you rotate or you'll countersink the hole.

safety warning

When using power tools, wear eye protection, remove any jewelry (including rings, bracelets, and necklaces), and tie back hair and any loose clothing. Read and follow the safety directions that come with your tool. Never bring the tool close to your body, hair, or clothing. If anything goes wrong, turn off the drill. If you have to adjust something close to the drill bit, turn off the power.

Using a Metal Punch

You don't need a drill to make holes in metal. Lots of punches and pliers can do a neat job. A punch like the style shown can make holes in two sizes in soft metals up to 18-gauge. When you turn the screw, a small dot of metal will fall out. Save these dots for scrap, to melt, or to solder in patterns for decoration.

Punches are limited by how far into a piece of metal they can reach; use a drill to make other sizes of holes or to reach where the punch can't.

Follow the steps below to use this type of punch.

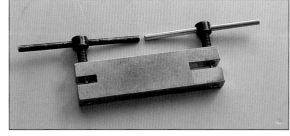

The black-handled screw on this EuroTool metal punch makes a ¹⁄₁₆-in. (1.6mm) hole and the silver makes a ³⁄₃₂-in. (2.4mm) hole.

1. Position the metal. Position the metal in the punch and tighten the screw. (For accurate placement, make a dot where the hole should be, turn the punch upside down, and look through the hole in the bottom, keeping the dot centered as you tighten the screw.)

2. Turn clockwise. Hold the punch in your palm and steady the metal with your fingers. Turn the handle clockwise, 1–2 revolutions, until the punch goes loose. Catch the dot that falls out.

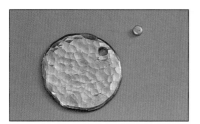

3. Reverse the punch. Turn the handle in the opposite direction to pull the screw out of the hole. If the dot of metal doesn't fall out, it's stuck in the punch. Tighten the screw again to push it out.

Using a Jeweler's Saw

The jeweler's saw is an essential tool. It is sharp enough to cut metal easily and agile enough to make sharp turns.

Load the saw blade into the frame so that it is taut; a loose blade is hard to control, difficult to saw with, and breaks easily. A taut blade flexes very little when pushed; when plucked sideways with a finger, it makes a short, high-pitched note.

You can saw free-form shapes or follow a sketched outline. Either draw right on the metal with permanent marker or draw a design on paper and glue it onto the metal with rubber cement. Let the glue dry for 5 minutes before sawing.

Jeweler's saw with V-slot bench pin and clamp.

HOW TO USE A JEWELER'S SAW

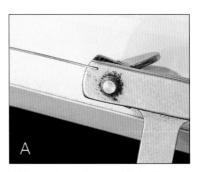

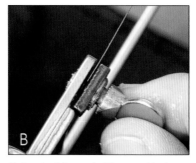

1. The teeth on the saw blade slant down toward the handle. Viewed from the side, the blade should look like a fir tree; it should feel smooth if stroked down toward the handle, and rough if stroked in the opposite direction. The teeth should face away from the back of the frame.

2. Place the top of the saw blade inside the top clamp, over the screw. Close the top clamp as tightly as you can by hand.

3. Adjust the frame to fit the blade. Loosen the clamp at the back of the frame and adjust the frame until ⅛ in.

(3.2mm) of the end of the saw blade overlaps the bottom clamp **[A]**. Tighten the back clamp and double-check that you still have ⅛ in. of blade to fit within the bottom clamp.

4. Open the bottom clamp. Rest the peg at the top of the frame on the table. Lean your upper body gently against the handle. Use a towel if you need more padding. Place the end of the saw blade inside the clamp, over the screw.

5. Tighten the saw frame. Hold the handle with one hand and lean gently forward against it. As the frame flexes, the blade will move further into the

clamp. Push it in about ¼ in. (6.4mm). Hold the tension on the frame and close the bottom clamp as tightly as you can **[B]**. Lean back slowly. If the blade is too tight, it will break when you lean back.

6. Check the tension. Pluck the blade with your finger. You should hear a high note and the blade should feel taut. If you press lightly against the blade, it should flex very little. If it flexes easily at your touch or while sawing, or makes a dull, low sound, it's too loose. Lean against the saw again, open the bottom clamp, push the blade farther in, and close the clamp again. If it loses tension as you saw, the clamps might not be

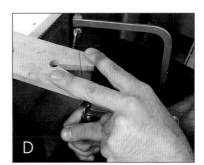

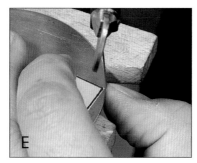

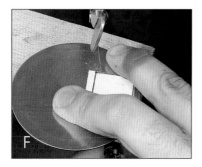

tight enough, or a piece of broken blade or other material may be in the clamp.

7. Use the saw frame with a V-slot bench pin. Sit with the open end of the V-slot pointing at your chest. Use the legs of the V-slot to support the metal while sawing inside the gap.

8. Lubricate the blade. Rub a block of paraffin or a beeswax candle periodically against the blade for easier sawing and to prolong the life of your blade **[C]**.

9. Hold the metal with two fingers. Use one finger over each leg of the V-slot. This position creates leverage that takes less strength and makes it easier to turn the metal as you saw. It's OK to reach through the saw frame **[D]**.

10. Make a notch. Start where the design is closest to the edge. To make a notch to get started, place your blade against the edge of the metal. Saw upward and back down, in a short stroke as if filing. Put your thumb on the smooth back of the blade to hold it steady while making the groove **[E]**.

11. Saw. Keep the saw blade perpendicular to the metal. Don't angle it forward or back or to the side. Sawing straight makes it easier to turn, and angling the blade can jam or break it.

Saw just outside your pattern **[F]**. Don't saw on the line because it's too easy to cut into your pattern. You can file back to the outline of your design later. Relax your grip; too much pressure will slow

down sawing and break the blade. Avoid flexing your wrist; sawing power comes from the elbow. To saw a curve, move the metal and not the saw blade.

12. Make sharp turns. To make a sharp turn, reduce your forward tension and gently saw up and down in place. Slowly turn the metal toward your new direction. This will grind a wide spot in the saw cut, allowing the blade to move. Keep the saw moving and don't twist the blade or it will break!

35

safety warning
Keep your fingers a safe distance from the front of the blade. Too close and you could saw through the metal and cut into your finger, or the broken tip of a blade could pierce your hand. Keep all of your fingers above the bench pin where you can see them.

Jump Rings

Buying quality jump rings can save you time and effort, but if you ever need a few rings in a pinch, it's good to know how to make your own. Use dowels, knitting needles, or a set of stepped mandrels to make coils of wire to cut into jump rings. If you know the outside diameter of the jump rings you want to make, subtract twice the millimeter thickness of the wire you're using, which will indicate the diameter of the mandrel to use. To trim the rings from the coil, use super-flush-cutters, which will provide the cleanest edge possible. Cheap cutters will leave a stepped cut, and the ring won't close completely.

MAKING JUMP RINGS

1. Coil. Hold 1 in. (2.5cm) of wire and wrap the rest around a mandrel. This short tail will give you a good grip on the wire while you wrap. Each full turn around the mandrel is a jump ring. Make a few extras and choose the best ones.

2. Trim excess wire. Remove the coil and cut off the short tail, leaving the end of the coil flush. Repeat on the other end to trim the rest of the wire.

3. Cut the jump rings. Flip the cutters over and align them with the end of the wire to cut the next ring in the coil. Only one jump ring should drop, and its ends should be flush. To cut subsequent rings, trim the wire end flush, reverse the cutters, and cut the ring free.

CLOSING JUMP RINGS FOR SOLDERING

It's much easier to solder a jump ring closed if the ends are aligned properly. The jump ring has to be closed so that if you hold it up to a light, you won't see light through the join. If the join is loose, the solder may flow away from it during subsequent soldering, or it may make a weak join that will break at some point. Follow these instructions for closing jump rings with tension for a tight fit.

1. Hold the jump ring with two pairs of pliers—one chainnose pliers and the other either flatnose or bentnose. The flatnose or bentnose pliers will do the bending. Don't cover too much of the jump ring with the pliers or they'll get in the way.

2. Open the jump ring by holding the chainnose pliers steady and making a small wrist movement to rotate the flatnose or bentnose pliers away from you.

3. Overlap the ends of the jump ring by pivoting your wrists and the pliers inward. When you bring the join together, the ends should overlap slightly.

4. Continue to close the jump ring, rubbing the ends over each other to create tension for a tight fit. You may hear a clicking sound. Hold the join up to the light. If you can see light through the join, repeat steps 1–4.

CORRECT ANY ALIGNMENT PROBLEMS

If the join is bad (for example, if one side is notched or beveled from a bad cut), no amount of work with the pliers will close it. Use a small, flat needle file to smooth the flaw. Use short strokes so you don't make the problem worse.

Using a Dapping Set

Dapping sets are conforming dies that dome (dap) metal disks. They have two parts: a block with graduated depressions and a matching set of round punches. You'll need a heavy hammer, such as a household ball-peen hammer, to hit the punches.

Dapping die sets come in wood, bronze, and steel. Bronze and wood are gentler on metal disks than steel. Steel can make the deepest domes. Using wood punches and a steel dapping block, or steel punches and a wood block, can shape your metal without losing texture. Buy the best dapping set you can afford that fits the style of jewelry you make. A quality block will have a large range of sizes and depths. Work on a cushion, such as a mouse pad, to soften the noise and protect the block.

Use a dapping die set to shape metal disks into domes. You can buy disks, saw them out of sheet metal, or punch them out using a disk cutter.

DAPPING

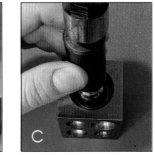
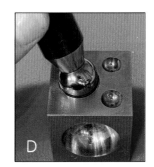

1. Find the right size dap. Find a depression that is a little larger than your metal disk **[A]**. (Starting too close to the same size as the disc will wrinkle the edges.) Make sure any texture is facing the right way—in most cases this would mean the textured side would be facing down.

2. Find a matching dapping punch. Choose a punch that is a little smaller than the same depression. There should be enough room for the thickness of the metal disk **[B]**. Using too large a punch will damage it.

3. Dap. Place your disk level inside the dap. Hold the punch in your nondominant hand, with your fingers below the end of the punch. Center the punch in the middle of the disk and hit it

with the hammer **[C]**. Tap the disk with firm blows; work quickly to shape the metal to the dome created by the dap; don't worry about any flat spots. Too much hammering can erase texture.

4. Repeat. Find the next deeper size dap that fits your disk and a matching punch. Repeat step 3 to make the dome the size and shape you want, or until you run out of daps that will fit. Don't use a dap that's too small; the edges of the concave shape will cut the metal.

5. Smooth the disk. Angle the disk or the punch in the dap and hammer out any flat spots or wrinkles **[D]**. If the metal gets stuck in the block, turn the block upside down and tap it with a hammer. The vibration should shake it loose.

Polishing Metal

After soldering, most metals are discolored with gray or red firescale. Soak the metal in pickle for 20 minutes or longer to remove as much firescale as possible, then remove any remaining firescale, excess solder, and scratches by polishing with sandpaper, files, or a rotary tool.

POLISHING BY HAND

The simplest way to polish your work is with files and sandpaper. Use needle files to remove excess solder and scratches and to refine the shape of your work. Finish with finer files to remove deeper file marks. Then use a 1-in. (2.5cm) strip of 400- or 600-grit sandpaper to remove fire stain and other discolorations from the surface. Sand across any scratches to remove them.

To bring up a shine on your metal, burnish with a brush that has fine brass bristles. Add a little hand soap to the bristles and occasionally dip the brush in water to lubricate it as you work. (A dry brass brush can smear a yellow tinge on silver, and the soap and water will help make a brighter polish.) Work over a tile or plastic mat or in a work sink. Scrub thoroughly, getting the bristles into every nook and cranny.

POLISHING WITH POWER TOOLS

Rotary tools for jewelry polishing should have 10 speeds from 5000–35000 rpm, a flex-shaft attachment, and a chuck accessory. They are available at most hardware stores as kits for under $100. I prefer models with direct power cords because batteries can die or slow down at the worst times—like in the middle of a job! The flex-shaft attachment is much more comfortable to hold while polishing than the larger rotary tool. The adjustable chuck will let you use a wider variety of bits, including drills. Hang the motor from a lightweight flex-shaft stand that clamps to your table.

Flex-shaft machines have a foot pedal that lets you control the speed while keeping your hands on your work. Their lightweight, interchangeable handpieces and wide selection of accessories make them an essential tool for a professional jewelry studio. They are available from jewelry suppliers and can cost $75 and up for an economy system, and $250 or more for a better quality tool with more power and control. Flex-shaft hangers made for these heavy motors can be clamped or screwed to your table. Because of the inherent ease of control, I like flex shafts more than rotary tools, and I recommend buying the best one that you can afford.

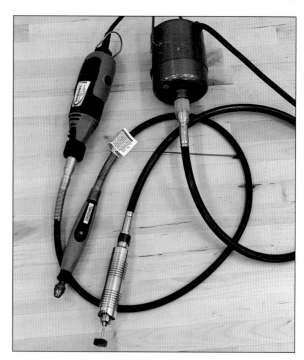

A rotary tool (left) can be fitted with an attachment that makes it comfortable to hold, much like a flex shaft (right). The flex shaft has a foot pedal for speed control.

POWER TOOL POLISHING TIPS

Hold the instrument properly. I hold the tool in my right (dominant) hand and the jewelry in my left hand. I dock my right thumb against the fingers of my left hand so that my hands are braced together. This way it's easy to stroke the polishing wheel against the metal as I curl the fingers on my right hand. It also controls how far forward the bit moves, so you can protect gemstones. If your arms are unsupported, you tend to have less control. Rest your hands, forearms, or elbows against the table. Adjust your chair or use a prop, such as a small box, to raise your work to a comfortable height.

Move the polishing wheels or bits toward you. With the handpiece in your right hand, the bit rotates clockwise or away from you, so move the tool toward you rather than away. If you're left-handed, this rotation can make it awkward. Some flex shafts allow you to reverse the rotation on the motor; most rotary tools don't have this feature.

Use the bottom edge of the wheel, not the face. Polishing with the face or flat plane of most wheels will break them and is harder to control. Instead, polish with the bottom edge of the wheel. Stroke the wheel in line with its edge or across the metal with the edge of the bit at a 45-degree angle.

Start in the middle and polish off the edges. When polishing, start with your wheel in the middle area of the piece and pull it toward you and off the edge. If you start on the far edge, the rotation of the tool can grab the piece and flip it out of your hand.

Sand across scratches. Sanding across a scratch will help you to see it disappear more clearly, because it will stand out against the texture from your polishing. If you sand in the same direction as a scratch, it hides itself in the texture, only to reappear when polishing with finer grits. Every time you switch to a finer grit, change direction with the bit to polish across the previous texture. Erase the old lines completely before moving on to the next step.

Blend with even pressure and move slowly. Polish with even pressure across the surface **[A]**. Don't leave dips and ripples. Drag the bit slowly to give it time to rotate against the metal. Polishing takes longer if you press too lightly or move too quickly. Use the right speed for the abrasive (see Properties of Polishing Abrasives chart on p. 41).

Don't polish away texture or details. Texture and details can disappear if you polish with coarse abrasives such as silicone wheels. Use less pressure and polish for a shorter amount of time. Use finer grits, such as 400-grit blue radial disks, and turn the tool so you are polishing in the direction of the texture **[B]**, not across it. Radial disks, which adapt to the surface, are good for texture and details.

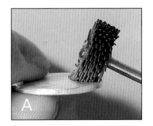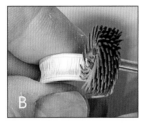

safety warning
When using power tools, always wear eye protection, remove any jewelry (including rings, bracelets, and necklaces), and tie back your hair or loose clothing. Read and follow the safety directions that come with your tool. Never bring the tool close to your body, hair, towels, or clothing. If anything goes wrong, turn it off. Wear a good quality dust mask. Never wear loose-fitting gloves, because they can get caught in the tool, either wrecking it or hurting you. When polishing chain or loose jewelry, do so by hand; forgo the power tools unless you get in-person training by an instructor.

USING POLISHING ABRASIVES

Polishing can be very messy. The dust from felt and bristle wheels charged with polishing compounds can stain your table, floors, and clothing. Split mandrels with sandpaper and abrasives, such as silicone polishing wheels, radial discs, and pin polishers, leave less debris to clean up. They come in progressively finer grits that you can use to polish jewelry to a mirror shine. Use the chart to compare the pros and cons of each one, to identify the order of the bits, and for advice on what speed to use. Don't work over your soldering area, including soldering tools such as boards and picks—polishing dust can contaminate them.

Split mandrels and sandpaper. Cut 1x4.25 in. (2.5x10.8cm) strips of sandpaper. Mount the mandrel in the chuck with the base as close to the teeth as possible. Thread the paper into the slot with the abrasive side facing you. The short end (about ¼ in./ 6.5mm) should be to the right of the mandrel and curled over slightly. When the tool is turned on low speed, the paper will curl around the bit. Press it against the metal until it forms a tight drum. Point the tip toward your left hand to turn the paper away from you so you aren't sanded too!

Silicone polishing wheels. Silicone polishers come in large and small wheels as well as cylinders for polishing rings. Wheels are available with flat edges for flat surfaces and knife edges to get into detailed areas. The coarse and medium wheels will remove metal and excess solder; they can also polish away details, such as hammer marks and texture, so take care when using them. They come without mandrels and have to be mounted on screw mandrels to use with your power tool. It doesn't matter which direction they're mounted.

Radial bristle disks. These flexible bristles can remove firescale and polish flat surfaces, wire, and textured surfaces to a beautiful finish. They are expensive, but they are very clean to work with and long lasting. Stack 3–6 disks on a screw mandrel with the curve of the bristles facing in the direction of the rotation of the tool. If they are facing the wrong way, they will bend backward and won't work as well. If you're using the power tool in your right hand, stack the disks with the manufacturer's stamp facing down.

Polishing pins. Thin cylinders of polishing abrasive fit into specially made mandrels that hold them securely in your rotary tool. Load the mandrel into the rotary tool chuck, then open the mandrel's chuck to insert, remove, raise, or lower the pin.

Split mandrels and sandpaper

Silicone polishing wheels

Radial bristle disks

Polishing pins

	PROPERTIES OF POLISHING ABRASIVES						
	PROS	CONS	SPEED	COARSE	MEDIUM	FINE	EXTRA-FINE
Split mandrels and sandpaper	Sands flat surfaces evenly. Easy to remove used paper to expose fresh abrasive. Fits inside rings, etc.	Rough on texture. Flattens details.	Slow	220-grit	320-grit	400- or 600-grit	1200-grit
Silicone polishing wheels	Good for flat surfaces, removing excess solder and scratches. White and black wheels can be shaped with a shaping block or old file to create different angles.	Can remove metal, texture, and distort jewelry, especially wire and flat surfaces.	Slow	White	Black	Blue	Pink
Radial bristle disks	Flexible bristles polish into texture and details with less distortion. Less friction and heat.	Harder to remove excess solder or reshape metal.	Medium	80-grit (yellow) to 120-grit (white)	220-grit (red)	400-grit (blue) to pumice (pink)	6μ (peach) to 1μ (light green)
Polishing pins	Round pins can be filed to a point or used flat to polish inside jump rings or bails.	Small surface area leaves track marks on your metal.	Slow	Dark Brown or Blue	Gray	Red	Green

USING A TUMBLER

Using a rotary tumbler can polish prepared pieces to a mirror shine and is a way to save time, especially when finishing lots of small parts. In the tumbler, mixed shapes of stainless steel shot burnish the metal, rubbing away fine scratches. But tumbling is not abrasive; it won't polish away deep scratches, firescale, excess solder, or file marks. For best results, remove those defects first by hand or with power tools, leaving the metal surface with a fine, satin finish.

For example, get to a 400-grit finish using sandpaper, blue radial discs, or black silicone polishing wheels. Use the brass brush to burnish a shine into the recesses. If you like, antique your pieces and neutralize them before tumbling (see Adding Patina, p. 42). Restore the highlights with polishing pads or by repeating the last step of polishing, and then tumble.

To prepare the tumbler, load the barrel with 1½–2 lb. (.7-.9kg) of mixed stainless steel shot. Add a tiny drop of dish soap or

A rotary tumbler with some stainless steel shot can make short work of your final polishing.

burnishing compound and just enough water to cover the surface of the shot. Add your pieces. Tumble for 20 minutes to 2 hours. Rinse with water. Your pieces will be burnished to a beautiful shine. Note: Tumbling can damage soft stones or beads, so tumble those pieces before adding stones or tumble for just a short time.

Adding Patina

Over time, metal jewelry—especially silver or copper pieces—will develop a patina. This may take years or perhaps only months if you live near the salty ocean air. If you like your pieces to be antiqued at a faster rate, perhaps with a patina in the recesses and polished highlights, you need to use a chemical to color the metal.

Liver of sulfur works exceptionally well on silver and copper, creating shades of color in addition to black. Silver Black and Black Max are used to add a black patina to silver or gold. Other patinas for specific metals, such as brass, are available from jewelry suppliers. Be aware that pickling, soldering, and excessive cleaning, polishing, or wear can remove patina. You can preserve patina for a time with Renaissance wax, light coats of spray varnish, or nail polish, but these topcoats may alter the patina.

LIVER OF SULFUR

Liver of sulfur (sometimes abbreviated LoS) is a mixture of potassium sulfides and is available as lumps, liquid, or gel. I especially like the new squirt-bottle gel, which means less exposure to the smell. When applied warm, LoS creates a range of colors from pale rose to black, especially on silver and copper. Unfortunately, it doesn't work as well on brass or gold.

Boil some water. Never heat LoS in your oven or microwave! Pour just enough hot water into a glass or plastic container to cover your jewelry. Add a small chunk of LoS (about the size of a pea is enough). The solution will be smelly and yellow-green in color. With tongs, tweezers, or a paper clip, dip or let the metal soak until it reaches the desired color. Rinse immediately in water. (You can also apply LoS solution with a swab, but it's a slower process.) Lighter colors such as yellow and blue can be made with a lukewarm or weak mix. These light patinas can change over time; you can always dip your piece in LoS again!

If you like an antique finish on your metal, you can use patina products such as Silver Black solution or liver of sulfur gel.

LoS that has been used but is still potent (still yellow-green) can be stored in a bottle with a tight-fitting lid. Store it in a dark place, since air and light make LoS lose its strength. Neutralize LoS solution by letting it sit exposed to sunlight until it turns clear or by adding baking soda to the solution—about 1 teaspoon per 2 cups solution. Do this outdoors or in an area with extra ventilation because the odor gets stronger. Dispose of neutralized solution at a hazardous waste facility.

SILVER BLACK AND BLACK MAX

These products, mixtures of hydrochloric acid and tellurium, immediately turn silver jewelry black. After the patina is applied and the silver is dark, neutralize it with a dip in water with baking soda. Unlike liver of sulfur, Silver Black and Black Max are used cold on silver. However, if you want to antique gold, you must heat the gold first and then dip the hot piece in the cold solution. Don't heat these products! Another option is to apply them with a steel brush. Steel will make a nasty vapor, so wear a respirator and work outside. Dip the piece into a small amount of solution in a plastic cup, or paint just the areas you want to patinate with a cotton swab. Use copper tongs or a plastic spoon to handle jewelry in the solution.

If metals other than jewelry metals (gold, copper, silver, and brass) are dipped in Silver Max or Black Max, it can release hydrogen gas into the air, with the potential for explosion. Do not pour this solution down drains, as it will corrode metal pipes and contaminate the water supply. Neutralize the used solution by pouring it into a larger container and adding baking soda—the solution will foam up. Silver Black and Black Max will stain stainless-steel counters and sinks. Carefully pour the rest back into the container when finished to use again later.

REMOVING PATINA

To accentuate texture, remove the patina from the highlights with a polishing pad or use a power tool, staying out of the recesses and polishing only the highlights. Leaving your piece in a patina solution for a long time will create a more durable patina, but it will take aggressive polishing or sanding to reveal the metal highlights. You may have to go back two or three polishing steps with radials (to pumice pink or 400-grit blue) or use fine blue or extra-fine pink silicone polishing wheels.

After removing patina from the highlights, you can tumble pieces in a rotary tumbler for a final finish. Make sure the pieces are completely neutralized so you don't contaminate the stainless steel shot. Check your piece every 5 minutes or so.

If your tumbler shot gets black and dirty, drain off the water and replace it with flat cola for a couple of hours to clean the shot. Rinse with water.

safety warning

Always read and follow the manufacturer's instructions and warnings, and follow basic safety rules: While using any patina solution, wear gloves and eye protection. Hang your piece from copper wire or use copper or bamboo tweezers or a disposable plastic spoon to handle your piece in the patina. Dispose of the solution according to the recommendations of the manufacturer. Never use food utensils to mix up patina solution and never prepare it in the same area where food is served or cooked. Take precautions to contain spills; work over a tray or inside a larger open container. Use in a ventilated area or outdoors. Keep all chemicals away from children and pets. Don't store your patina solution near metal, chain, or tools, because it will discolor them.

Grease and dirt will interfere with the patination process, so make sure your piece is clean. Set up a glass or plastic cup for the patina solution, another cup for rinse water, a third cup with water and baking soda to neutralize the solution, and a fourth cup for a final rinse. The first rinse cup will absorb some patina but won't stop the reaction.

Tool & Equipment Sets

To help you prepare for making the projects, review these lists. Most projects call for the basic sets plus a few specialty tools, which will be listed in the box at the start of each project. There you'll also find the recommended size of butane torch—micro or jumbo.

Basic Sets

SOLDERING

- Micro butane torch
- Jumbo butane torch
- Titanium soldering pick
- Stainless steel 6–8-in. (15.2–20.3cm) nonlocking tweezers
- Third hand base
- Cross-locking tweezers with fiberboard handles
- Tripod with steel mesh
- Large ceramic tile(s)
- Solder board
- Compressed charcoal block
- Bowl filled with water
- Paste flux
- Firescoff flux
- Biodegradable citric pickle
- Pickle pot (small electric crock)
- Copper pickle tongs
- Inexpensive craft paintbrush

FORGING

- Unpolished or household hammers: 8-oz. ball-peen, chasing
- Polished hammers: cross-peen or goldsmith, ball-peen
- Polished steel bench block
- Rawhide mallet

PLIERS

- Chainnose pliers
- Flatnose pliers
- Roundnose pliers
- Flat/half-round bending and forming pliers
- Flush-cutters

TRIMMING/FILING/DRILLING

- Jeweler's saw frame
- V-slot bench pin with clamp
- French shears
- Needle files (economy set of 12)
- Medium-cut 6-in. (15.2cm) large half-round file
- File cleaning card
- Ring clamp
- Center punch
- Two-hole metal punch
- Rotary tool, handheld drill, or drill press
- Drill bits: $\frac{1}{16}$ in. (1.5mm) or smaller
- Saw blades: size 2/0 or 4/0

POLISHING/PATINATING

- Wet/dry sandpaper for metal: 320- and 600-grit
- Rotary tool or flex shaft
- Attachments: radial disks (white/120-grit to light green/1µ), pin polishers, silicone polishing wheels, split and screw mandrels
- Tumbler
- Liver of sulfur gel or Silver Black
- Baking soda

UTILITY

- Fine-point permanent marker
- Ruler with inches and metric
- Piece of soft leather or cloth

Specialty Tools

- Metal design and chasing stamps
- Large cupped nail set stamp (from hardware store)
- Curved steel burnisher
- Dapping block and punches (wood or steel)
- Dividers
- Tapered steel ring mandrel with sizes marked

PART TWO
Projects

Now let's have some fun!

In this section, you'll find 12 jewelry projects that get you right into some hands-on torch work. We'll start simply, with some easy-to-make yet custom-looking ear wires. Consider setting a goal to complete each project in order. By the time you finish the final project, the layered pendant, you'll be experienced and confident at jewelry soldering.

Custom Ear Wires

This project will show you how to melt sterling silver into small disks, head pins, and decorative balls, and how to solder them together to make custom earrings. These basic skills form the building blocks for later projects.

techniques

Melting metal
Making head pins
Basic soldering
Sweat-soldering

tools

Soldering, pliers, polishing, and utility sets plus polished hammer, bench block, flat file
Micro butane torch

materials

12 in. (30.5cm) of 20-gauge sterling round wire
Easy sterling solder
Beads and wire for dangles

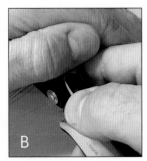

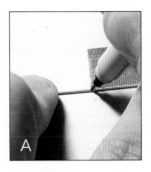

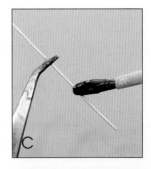

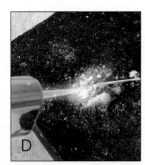

A B C D

STEP 1: MAKE TWO DISKS AND TWO BALLS

With a fine-point permanent marker, mark a length of 20-gauge sterling round wire at 2½ in. (64mm) and 5 in. (12.7cm) **[A]**. Shielding the end of the wire with your hand, cut the wire at both marks **[B]** Using flux will help minimize firescale, so apply a thin, even coat to the entire wire with an inexpensive paintbrush **[C]**.

Although you could use either size of torch for this project, the micro torch is well-suited to delicate work like making earrings and ear wires.

Place the two pieces of wire on a charcoal block at least 1 in. (25.5mm) apart. Don't let them touch or they'll melt into one large ball! Use a hot, pointed, oxidizing flame to melt each wire into a round ball. Bring the tip of the blue cone inside the flame very close to the surface of the wire. Warm the length of the metal a few times, back and forth. As the silver heats, it will start to glow red. Hold the flame on one end of the metal as it glows red and starts to look molten, with the flame also pointing down the rest of the wire. This will preheat the rest of the wire and help you melt it faster **[D]**. Continue heating, following the wire as it balls up, until it pulls up into a round, wiggling ball **[E]**. Remove the heat but don't move the ball.

Move to the second wire and make a second silver ball. After both balls turn from red-hot to black, pick them up with tweezers. Flux can make a ball stick to the block; warm it gently with your torch to loosen the flux. (If you pry it up, you'll take chunks of charcoal with it.) Quench. Place the balls in pickle.

Cut two pieces of 20-gauge wire, each ¼ in. (6.5mm) long. Melt each into a very small ball. If you're not pleased with the shape or texture of a ball, you can melt it again. Since it was melted on a flat block, the bottom of the ball will be flat (which is fine for this design).

E

47

F

Quench the balls. Let all of the balls pickle for 10–15 minutes. Rinse in water. The balls may look a little black, pink, or coppery after pickling. This is firescale, but don't worry; a little polishing will remove that later.

Dry the large sterling balls. Using a steel block and a polished hammer with a slightly rounded face, flatten them to about ¹⁄₁₆ in. (1.6mm) thick **[F]**. Hammer both sides of each disk.

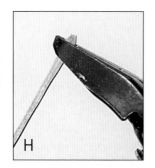

STEP 2: SWEAT-SOLDER THE BALLS TO THE DISKS

The disks and balls will be the decoration for the earrings. You'll use a two-step, sweat-soldering technique to join them. To make it easier to apply the solder, first hammer flat ½ in. (13mm) of easy sterling solder wire **[G]**. Use the flush (flat) side of your cutters to cut two chips, about ⅟₁₆ in. (1.6mm) square or smaller **[H]**. Flux them lightly **[I]**.

The flux should be thin like pancake batter and free of lumps. If it's too thick and pasty, mix in a little water with your brush to thin it. If it's too watery, mix up thick flux from the bottom of the jar. Rinse any excess flux on the brush in your water cup.

Completely flux both sides of the disks and the silver balls **[J]**. Place the balls upside down 1 in. apart on the solder board, with any flat spots facing up. Warm one ball with a neutral flame until the flux turns clear. Remove the heat and use nonlocking steel tweezers to place a chip of easy solder on top of the ball **[K]**. The flux must be warm and tacky for the solder to stick. Continue heating until the solder melts flat to the surface **[L]**. The ball will glow pale red when the solder flows.

Place the ball, solder side down, on the disk and heat them together until the solder flows again **[M]**. The solder will look like a ring of molten silver around the bottom of the ball. Have a solder pick handy to adjust the ball if it moves. To reposition the ball, bring the piece back up to light red and when the solder is molten again, slide it with the pick. Repeat for the second ball and disk. Quench, pickle for 5 minutes, and rinse.

STEP 3: MAKE SOME HEAD PINS

You'll make the ear wires from ball head pins made with the torch. (You can also make more head pins to use for the earrings' bead dangles if you like.) Trim the end of the 20-gauge wire flat with flush-cutters. Measure 2½ in. from the flush end, mark it, and cut the other end flush, too. Repeat for a second piece. Straighten the wires with your fingers or nylon-jaw pliers. Hold the wire with steel tweezers and flux the whole piece. The flux will keep the rest of the wire clean while the end is heated to form a ball.

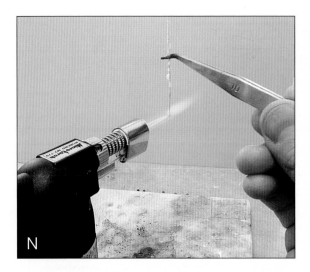

Set the wire on the solder board. Light the torch and adjust it to create an oxidizing flame with a sharp cone. Pick up the fluxed wire with tweezers. Hold the torch steady on the table with the flame pointed away from the tweezers and away from your hand. Keep the wire vertical and move the bottom end down into the flame, just in front of the tip of the cone [N]. Keep the heat on the tip until it draws up into a ball. As soon as it reaches the size you want, remove the heat. If the ball is off center, reheat it. When it gets shiny and molten again, tilt the wire to center the ball and quickly remove the heat. If the ball is wrinkled or deformed, heat it again. Quench and pickle. Make a second head pin, quench, and pickle both pieces for 5–15 minutes. Rinse.

STEP 4: SOLDER THE DISKS TO THE HEAD PINS

Mark each head pin with a permanent marker ¼ in. from the ball. (This will leave enough room for a small loop later.) Completely flux a head pin and place it on the solder board. It should lie straight and flat against the board. Flux both sides of one of the soldered disks from step 2. Place the flat side on the wire, with the bottom edge on the marked line [O]. Make sure the disk is centered. Cut and flux 2–3 flat chips of easy solder. Warm the wire and disk with a neutral flame until the flux turns clear. Use tweezers or a pick to place a chip of solder where the disk meets the wire. Warm the top of the head pin above the disk first [P]. As the flux clears, direct the flame at the side of the disk away from the solder, so the heat will draw the solder through the join. Heat the disk and wire together. They should both glow pale red just as the solder flows into the join along the bottom of the disk [Q]. If they glow bright red or orange, you're overheating them!

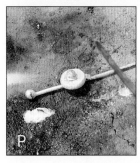

Repeat for the second earring. Quench, pickle for 20 minutes or longer to remove as much firescale as possible, and rinse.

An option is to sweat-solder the disk to the head pin. First melt a chip of easy solder on the wire where the disk will sit. Center the disk on the wire, over the solder. Heat all the silver evenly. The disk and the wire should glow a pale red. Look for the disk to settle as the solder flows or watch for signs of molten solder along the edges of the join. Quench, pickle and rinse. You should see a line of solder along the wire on the back of the disk.

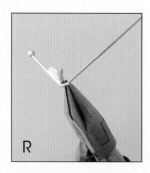 R

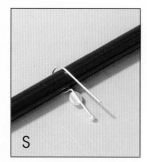 S

 T

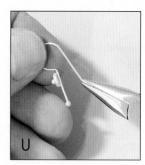 U

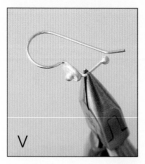 V

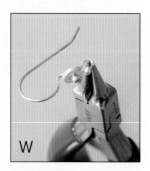 W

 X

STEP 5: FORM THE EAR WIRES

Use chainnose pliers to make a right-angle bend toward the front or disk side of the ear wire, close to the top of the disk **[R]**. Bend the wire back, around a round mandrel, such as the handle of your solder pick **[S]**. This will form the loop **[T]**. Bend the last ⅛ in. (3.2mm) of the wire 45 degrees with chainnose pliers **[U]**. Bend the ball end 90 degrees, just below the disk **[V]**. Switch to roundnose pliers and, working near the tips, roll the wire into a loop with the ball touching the disk **[W]**. Forge the round loop flat to work-harden it so it holds its shape **[X]**. The wire should be not too thin and it should be wider in the middle and taper toward the disk as well as the tail end **[Y]**. Repeat for the second ear wire. If the wire ends are sharp, smooth them with a flat needle file or a cup bur.

STEP 6: ADD DANGLES

Add bead dangles to transform your ear wires into earrings!

> **tip**
> This ear wire style can be used in many earrings. Want something even easier? Simply skip the disks!

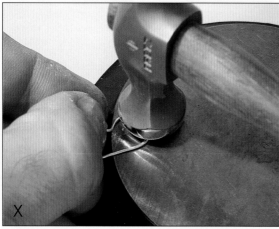 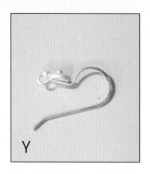 Y

Lily Pad Post Earrings

Making these earrings
will give you some soldering
practice and introduce
you to some new skills: filing
metal into custom shapes,
texturing with a hammer,
dapping a flat disk into
a dome, and using a
third hand.

techniques
Melting metal
Filing
Dapping
Basic soldering
Sweat-soldering

tools
All tool sets plus steel dapping
block, wooden punch
Micro or jumbo butane torch

materials
2 24-gauge ½ in. (13mm) diameter sterling disks
¾ in. (19mm) of 20-gauge sterling round wire
2 20-gauge 5mm outside diameter (OD) jump rings
2 sterling earring posts
Easy sterling solder
Beads and wire for dangles

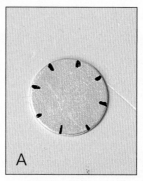

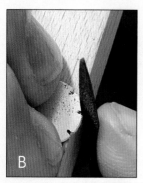

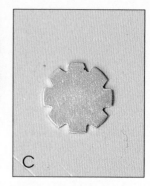

STEP 1: MAKE TWO LILY PADS FROM DISKS

Mark a disk with a permanent marker as shown to define the eight petals of the lily pad **[A]**. Rest the disk on a wooden bench pin clamped to your table and make a shallow notch at each mark with a triangular needle file **[B]**. Continue filing to make deeper notches to separate the petals **[C]**. To round the square shapes, file a 45-degree angle on the corners with a flat needle file. Smooth the corners into curves **[D]**. To smooth the edges, turn the disk sideways and file at an angle across them to remove nicks and deep file marks.

Place the disk in the center of a steel bench block. Use a cross peen hammer to make long planish marks that radiate from the center **[E]**. Move from the center toward the edge and rotate the disk slowly as you hammer. To slightly dome the disk while retaining much of the texture, use a steel dapping block, a wooden punch, and an unpolished steel hammer, such as a chasing hammer **[F]**. Repeat for the second disk to make two lily pads.

STEP 2: SWEAT-SOLDER THREE SILVER BALLS INSIDE EACH DOME

Cut six ⅛-in. (3.2mm) pieces of 20-gauge sterling wire. Melt each one separately into a ball on a charcoal block. Quench, pickle for 10–15 minutes, and rinse.

Completely flux one of the disks and place it texture side up on the charcoal block. Hammer flat 1 in. (25.5mm) of easy solder wire. Cut and flux two small chips. Heat the disk with a neutral flame until the flux clears. With your tweezers, place one chip of solder in the center of the disk. Continue heating, using the solder pick to keep the solder in place **[G]**, until it melts into a small puddle. Add three silver balls to the solder, placing the flat sides down. Heat until the silver glows light pink and the solder flows again, attaching the balls **[H]**. Quench, pickle for

5 minutes, and rinse. Check your work to make sure the balls are soldered in place. Repeat for the second disk.

STEP 3: ATTACH JUMP RINGS

Prepare the jump rings for soldering by closing them tightly with two pair of pliers. Hold a ring with tweezers, flux all sides, and place it on the solder board. Cut and flux a few small, flat chips of easy solder. Warm the ring with a neutral flame until the flux turns clear. Move the flame aside and place a chip of solder on the join with tweezers. Switch to the pick, in case the solder moves while you work. Continue heating the ring and the solder until the silver turns light pink and the solder flows into the join **[I]**. Repeat for the second jump ring. Quench, pickle, and rinse.

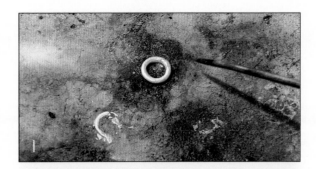

With a permanent marker, mark the backs of the lily pads where you want to attach jump rings. Cut and flux another 2–3 small, flat chips of easy solder. Flux both sides of one lily pad, and place it face down on the charcoal block. Place the jump ring on the marked petal, with the join facing the middle of the lily pad. Heat both pieces until the flux turns clear. Place one chip of solder on the join, touching the ring and the lily pad **[J]**. Continue heating both pieces until the solder flows and attaches the jump ring. Repeat for the second lily pad. Quench, pickle, and rinse.

STEP 4: SWEAT-SOLDER THE POSTS TO THE BACKS

Attaching a post to an earring can be tricky, since you have to center the post and apply solder while you keep it in place. Two tips will make this job easier: 1) Use a third hand to hold the jump ring in place, and 2) Sweat-solder the post to the earring.

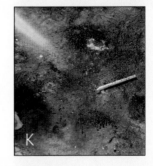

Cut and flux 2–3 small, flat chips of easy solder. Completely flux the post and place it on the solder board. Warm the flux until it turns into a clear glaze. Place a small, flat chip of easy solder on the tip away from the grooved end **[K]**. Continue heating until the solder melts to the tip **[L]**. Repeat for the second post. Let them cool on the board as you prepare the earring backs.

53

> **tip**
> To melt silver wire into a perfectly round ball, make a shallow divot on the charcoal with a small round dapping punch, and melt the silver in the depression.

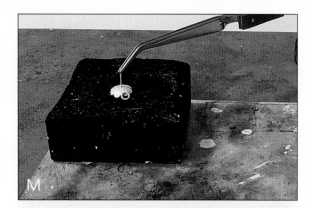

Mark the back of each earring to help you position the posts. Completely flux one of the lily pad disks. Place it face down on the charcoal block. Pick up a post with tweezers and place it in cross-locking tweezers attached to a third-hand base. Hold the end away from solder with the tips of the tweezers **[M]**. Center the other end on the back of the disk, matching it to the dot. Make sure the end of the post is flush to the pad **[N]**. There should still be a glaze of flux baked on the post from previous steps, but if in doubt, add a little more flux to the post.

Flux is unstable. If you leave flux on metal too long before working with it (say 5 minutes or longer), the glaze will start to crack and fall off, exposing silver.

To get the solder to flow from the post to the lily pad disk, heat the two pieces evenly. The small, light post will heat faster than the domed disk and the solder could flow up the post. Don't focus the flame on the join; instead, heat the disk, which will take longer to warm up. Then, as the flux clears even more and the silver turns a matte white color bordering on a light pink glow, move the flame to the join and watch the solder flow **[O]**. Repeat for the second earring. Quench the earrings, pickle for 20 minutes or longer, and rinse. Any firescale or defects can be removed with polishing.

STEP 5: ADD DANGLES
Attach bead dangles to the jump rings to finish your earrings.

Jump Ring Flower Earrings

This project uses jump rings and wire to make a pair of earrings. You'll practice moving smaller amounts of solder with a pick as well as evenly heating pieces of different thicknesses. The techniques taught in this project transfer to many variations of pendants, links, toggles, and so on.

techniques

Pick-soldering
Soldering jump rings
Fabricating with solder
Sweat-soldering
Soldering thick and thin parts

tools

All tool sets
Micro or jumbo butane torch

materials

6 in. (15.2cm) of 18-gauge sterling round wire
8 6mm OD 18-gauge sterling jump rings
2 4mm OD 20-gauge sterling jump rings
Easy sterling solder
Ear wires
Beads and wire for dangles

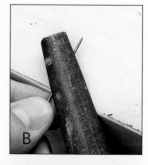

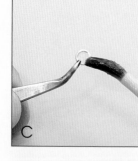

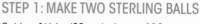

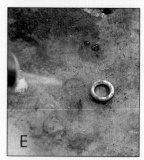

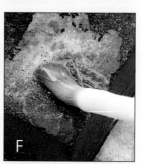

STEP 1: MAKE TWO STERLING BALLS

Cut two 1¼-in. (32mm) pieces of 18-gauge sterling round wire. Flux both wires and place them about 2 in. (51mm) apart on a charcoal block. Melt both pieces into round balls with flat bottoms **[A]**. Quench. Soak the balls in pickle while you solder the jump rings.

STEP 2: SOLDER EIGHT JUMP RINGS

Prepare eight 6mm 18-gauge jump rings for soldering by completely closing them with two pair of pliers. Use your pick to place tiny balls of solder on these small seams. Using just enough solder to close the join results in a better-looking jump ring and less polishing.

Use a file to clean the pick of any sticky, baked-on flux or solder **[B]**. Pick up each closed jump ring with tweezers by the side opposite the join and completely flux it **[C]**. Place each jump ring on the solder board, leaving 1 in. (25.5mm) between them, with the joins at 2 o'clock for right-handers and 10 o'clock for lefties.

Use the torch to ball up a small chip of fluxed easy solder, move the flame aside, and scoop up the solder with the pick. Warm a jump ring until the flux turns clear and, as you hold this temperature, place the solder on the join line **[D]**. To solder the jump ring, warm the side away from the join first, and then bring the heat to the join **[E]**. Remember, if your heat

is uneven, the solder will flow to hottest side. Position the flame so the heat is directed through a virtual line down the middle of the jump ring and through the join. As soon as the solder flows flat to the silver, remove the heat and move the jump ring aside to cool. Repeat for the remaining seven rings. Quench, pickle, and rinse.

STEP 3: SOLDER THE RINGS TOGETHER

Pieces you want to join may move apart while placing solder, and that can be frustrating. Take advantage of the way flux glues pieces to charcoal and solder board to hold the parts right where you want them!

Make sure there is enough flux to hold the rings in place by painting a thin coat of flux on a flat spot on the charcoal **[F]**. (If you can see a glossy patch of old flux, more is probably not necessary; the flux will get sticky again when heated.) Flux four of the soldered rings as before, and place them in a flower

pattern as shown **[G]**. Place the joins toward the center of the pattern. Cut and flux 4–6 small chips of easy solder, but don't flatten them. Warm the rings and the charcoal block with a neutral flame **[H]**. As the flux clears, if any rings move, use the pick to nudge them back into place.

Simmer the heat by moving the flame farther away until the flux on the charcoal also turns clear. Don't overheat the rings! You shouldn't see them glow any shade of red or the solder in their joins will melt. Move the flame to the solder chips and pick up one of the chips. In the time it takes to ball up and scoop a solder chip, the flux on the jump rings will cool and harden. With only a bare brush of the flame, place a ball of solder between two rings. Repeat for all four joins **[I]**. After all four solder balls are in place, bring the flame closer and move in a slow circle above the rings until the solder starts to flow. Then focus on each join in turn **[J]**. Repeat for the second set of four jump rings. Remember to use the flame to loosen the flux after soldering so that you can remove the earring without bending it out of shape. Quench, pickle, and rinse.

Timing is important. If you take too long joining the jump rings, the flux will crack and the solder may pop off. If you use too much heat while applying the solder, the rings will loosen and move apart. Just nudge them back into place with the pick while you warm the flux with the torch. The goal of this project is to develop enough control to place all four balls of solder first and melt them afterwards. If that's too difficult, you can place and solder one pair of rings at a time.

STEP 4: SWEAT-SOLDER THE SILVER BALLS

Sweat-soldering the silver balls to the center of the ring pattern is the easiest and cleanest way to solder this join. If you place chips of solder around the ball, they might flow to the ball and not into the join, or they might flow to the jump rings. Even if this works, the solder will first melt to

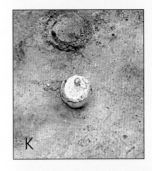

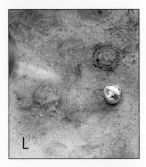

the surface of the rings and then flow into the join, leaving a trail of solder behind.

Prepare the pieces for soldering by fluxing the ring pattern and balls thoroughly. Place the rings face up on the charcoal block. Put the ball upside down with the flat side up on the solder board. Warm the ball with a neutral flame; when the flux turns clear, place a ball of solder on the flat spot **[K]**. Continue heating until the solder melts **[L]**. Flip the ball over with tweezers and place it solder side down in the center of the rings **[M]**.

Warm the entire piece with the torch, making any final adjustments as the flux settles and clears. Continue heating until you see signs of sweat-soldering: The ball may shift down as the solder melts, or molten solder may appear around the edge of the ball. Direct the heat at the entire piece: ball and rings evenly. You should see a light pink glow on the silver when the solder flows **[N]**. Repeat for the second set of rings and ball. Quench, pickle, and rinse.

STEP 5: ATTACH THE SMALL JUMP RING AND LEAVES

The ear wires will attach to 4mm 20-gauge jump rings you'll solder to the top of the flower pattern. At the bottom, forged and bent 18-gauge wires form the "leaves" and a loop for a bead dangle.

Cut two 1-in. (25.5mm) pieces of 18-gauge wire, flush-cutting both ends. Use a hammer with a slightly round face and the steel bench block to forge one-third of the wire into a paddle end **[O]**. Leave the center third round. Repeat on the other end to make two parallel paddle ends **[P]**.

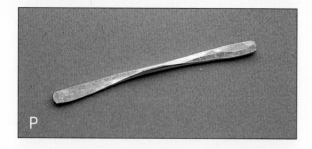

As you hammer, the metal gets wider and thinner. Hammer more toward the end and less toward the middle to make the paddle. Don't thin the metal too much, or it will be too weak. If the wire starts to curve, you're hammering more on one edge, causing it to grow and bend. Hammer along the edge on the inside of the curve to straighten it.

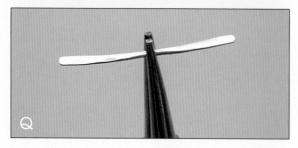

File the ends round with the flat side of a file to remove any jagged edges. Hold the middle of the wire with the tips of roundnose pliers **[Q]**. Using your fingers, bend one end back toward the other at a 45-degree angle **[R]**. Bend the other end under or over the first at a 45-degree angle in the opposite direction **[S]**. Check the fit against the bottom jump ring of a flower and make any adjustments so that the leaves touch in two places for soldering. The slight twist created when you bent the wire should help. Repeat for the second flower-and-leaves set. Flux all four components completely and set them aside.

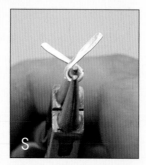

Close the 20-gauge jump ring, flux it, and solder it closed **[T]**. Since this ring is tiny, use the smallest piece of solder that you can scoop up—and be gentle with the flame!

The flux on the charcoal that held the pieces together should still be usable, so place the fluxed flower there. Place the small jump ring with its join against the top ring in the flower. Warm them together until the flux turns clear. Simmer the heat until you see that the flux on the charcoal also looks glossy and wet. Scoop up a small ball of easy solder while the earring cools for 10–20 seconds. With the barest brush of the flame, place the solder on the join between the rings. Turn the flame so you are heating from the side, with most of the heat on the flower **[U]**. This will help avoid overheating the little ring as you solder.

If you direct all the heat at the join or the small ring, the solder will flow to this thin piece and away from the join. Instead, heat mostly the thickest part, the rings and ball, and watch the solder. If it starts to move toward the thick center of the flower, move the heat to the small ring to get it to flow into the join. If it moves toward the small ring, you need more heat on the flower.

Place one of the fluxed wire leaf components against the bottom ring of the flower. Warm the pieces together until the flux clears on the leaves, then let them cool briefly while you scoop up a ball of easy solder. Place the ball at one of the joins between the leaves and the flower. The leaf component looks wide and thick, but it's actually thin from forging; if it gets too hot, all the solder will flow to the leaves and coat the silver.

Bring the flame in from the side again, heating mostly the flower. By heating the thickest part first, you'll let the flower catch up to the thinner leaves, and the solder will flow more easily into the join **[V]**. Place a second ball of solder on the second join **[W]** and solder it closed. If the second join is too open to solder, quench the earring and bend the leaf into place. Soldering the first join tacked the wire in place and softened it, so it should be easy to bend. Flux again and solder. Repeat for the second earring. Quench, pickle for 20 minutes or longer, rinse, and polish.

STEP 6: ADD DANGLES

Attach the flowers to ear wires and finish with bead dangles.

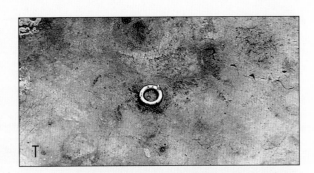

Soldering Clasps, Charms, & Beaded Rings

Attaching findings such as clasps and charms by soldering makes your jewelry more valuable as well as more secure! You'll learn how to solder next to chain links and to isolate heat from delicate materials such as beads.

techniques

Soldering chain
Attaching charms and clasps
Soldering near delicate materials

tools

All tool sets plus third hand
    with cross-locking tweezers
Micro butane torch

materials

16–18 in. (40.6–45.7cm) sterling chain with long-and-short
    soldered links
12 in. (30.5cm) 18-gauge sterling wire
2 large-hole rondelle beads
2 6mm OD 18-gauge sterling jump rings
Sterling lobster claw clasp
Sterling charm
Easy sterling solder

A

STEP 1: CONNECT CHAIN, CLASP, AND CHARM

You'll connect the parts for the necklace before soldering to test the design and fit. This project creates a necklace that's about 16 in. (40.6cm) long, but you are welcome to alter that length.

Out of the 18-gauge sterling wire, make three jump rings: two 12mm, and one 8mm. Cut a 1⅞–2½ in. (48–64mm) length of sterling chain with closed links at both ends. Attach the charm to the chain's center with a 6mm jump ring so the pattern of links is symmetrical on either side of the charm.

Attach a 12mm ring to each end of the center chain and add a large-hole bead to each ring. The beads should fit loosely on the large rings yet be small enough to leave space between the bead and the join. Connect a 6¼–6½-in. (15.9–16.5cm) length of chain to the large rings on each side and close the rings. Connect the 8mm jump ring to one end of the chain and use a 6mm jump ring to connect the lobster claw clasp to the other end.

Test the fit of the assembled necklace and make any adjustments so that the beads hang evenly, the charm hangs correctly, and the chain is not twisted **[A]**. Close each open jump ring tightly to prepare for soldering.

B

STEP 2: SOLDER LINKS FOR CLASP AND CHARM

Start with the 8mm jump ring at the end of the necklace. Flux the jump ring and a few links of chain that could be exposed to heat. The flux will keep the chain clean and, if it isn't glazed by the heat, will rinse off in water.

For simple connections like this, where the ring is at the end, you can use the charcoal block to boost the heat from the torch for quick soldering: Lay a section of the chain on the block with the join of the ring positioned as far away from the next link as possible. Scoop up a ball of easy solder. Point the flame in the direction of the join and away from the chain. Heat the jump ring with a hot, oxidizing flame until the flux turns clear. Simmer the silver at this temperature, before it turns pink or red, as you place the solder on the join. Continue heating until the solder flows **[B]**.

BEAD MATERIAL RATINGS			
DURABLE	NORMAL	DELICATE	AVOID
Cubic zirconia	Ceramic	Coated	Amber
Diamonds	Crystal	Opal	Fabric
Rubies	Glass	Pearls	Pewter
Sapphires	Stone	Plated	Plastic
			Resin
			Wood

Some materials are too delicate to endure the heat of soldering. This table rates various materials of beads for this project. Coatings on beads (particularly crystals) and plating on metal (such as vermeil) can burn off if exposed to heat for too long. Materials that melt or ignite at low temperatures—plastic, pewter, resin, and wood—should be avoided at least until you master this technique.

Soldering jump rings between links, or between a clasp and a link, is a bit more complicated. If you try to solder this type of connection with the ring flat on a block, as above, a few frustrating things can happen: The jump ring can move easily, pushing the join too close to the chain links, and the links can become fused in a stiff pattern. Or delicate mechanisms, such as the steel spring inside a lobster claw clasp, can be overheated and stop working. Instead, use cross-locking tweezers and a third-hand base to solve this problem! The cold steel of the tweezers is a heat sink; whatever it holds will take longer to heat or solder.

Move to the jump ring attaching the lobster claw to the necklace. Since we want to solder this ring quickly, use tweezers in the third hand to hold the links and clasp **[C]**. The jump ring should be loose enough to move easily, if pushed with your pick, but tight enough to stand up straight, with the join at the top, away from the tweezers **[inset]**. Tug down on the clasp and chain to adjust the tension. If it's too tight and can't move, it will slow your soldering down, potentially damaging the clasps or links below.

After the tweezers are in position, flux the jump ring, the clasp, the link in the tweezers, and a few links of the chain below **[D]**. Use a sharp, oxidizing flame to scoop up a ball of easy solder and then heat the jump ring until the flux turns clear. Keep the flame parallel to the table or pointing slightly upward, always away from the clasp and chain below. Keep the jump ring warm while you place the solder on top of the join **[E]**. Bring the point of the blue cone of the flame very close to the jump ring. Heat it evenly, including the sides of the jump ring, until the solder flows. If the solder is taking too long to flow, loosen the tension on the jump ring by moving it back and forth with your pick.

This technique is a great example of why I say that titanium picks make for happy soldering. Solder won't melt onto a titanium pick, even if the pick is red hot. But common steel picks will overheat, the solder will melt onto the pick, and it won't come off—and this will happen over and over again.

Repeat these steps to close the jump ring attaching the charm to the chain. Hold the charm and the links in the tweezers, and raise the link to be soldered, as shown **[F]**.

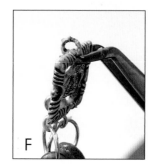

Charms made of jewelry metals that are safe to solder (silver, copper, and gold) are very durable, although you may lose some patina or polish. Isolating the charm from the heat will make finishing the necklace faster. If the charm gets discolored during soldering, a quick soak in pickle will usually clean it.

Quench and pickle the necklace. Be sure the pickle is steaming hot and soak it for only a minute or two. Only the flux on the jump rings was hardened by the heat, so it will come off very quickly. Long soaks in the pickle can damage patina, polish, and even some beads.

STEP 3: SOLDER JUMP RINGS WITH BEADS

Whenever possible, try to arrange your workflow so that you avoid soldering close to delicate materials, particularly beads. For example, if you are making a charm bracelet with wire-wrapped beads, plan to solder the chain, clasps, and charms first, pickle and polish the piece, and add the wire-wrapped beads last.

That said, there are a few ways to isolate beads from the heat and still solder successfully. Make sure the bead is loose on the jump ring. If the bead is tight, it will be easier to overheat. Choose a bead that's small enough to leave space to heat the join without also heating the bead. Use 16-gauge or finer jump rings so your torch can heat them quickly. And try to break the conduction of heat to the bead by holding it with a third hand or even two third hands. Choose inexpensive beads for practice until you master this skill.

Hold one of the large jump rings with the tips of the third-hand tweezers, as far from the join as possible. Pull any beads and links close to the tweezers. Rest the jump ring on a charcoal block to help boost the heat from your torch. Flux the jump ring, bead, and a few links of chain. The flux on the bead and chain will act as an alarm—if the flux on the bead starts to bubble and turn clear, it's getting too hot!

Use a hot, pointed oxidizing flame and a full torch to warm the jump ring and place the solder. Always point the flame away from the bead! In this instance, direct the flame over and past the bead to heat the join. Notice that the hottest spot is on the far side of the jump ring [G]. Try to solder the jump ring as quickly as possible. If you take too long, the heat can reach the bead and crack it. Repeat for the second large ring and bead. Do not quench your pieces, which could crack the beads! Delicate beads, such as pearl, opal, amber, and turquoise, should not be pickled. Whenever in doubt, hold those beads above the solution and pickle only the part of the jump ring that was soldered. It should take less than a minute in hot pickle to clean. Any unbaked flux will rinse away in water.

STEP 4: TEXTURE JUMP RINGS
Dry the necklace completely to avoid rusting steel tools. Rest one of the large links flat on the bench block and texture with a polished ball-peen hammer [H]. The texture will strengthen the ring and add interest to your design [I]. Repeat on both sides, for both rings.

STEP 5: FINISHING
Most jump rings will need only light polishing. Use a blue 400-grit radial disk to remove any scratches or firescale. Blend those rings up to the same polish as the rest of the necklace, with progressively finer disks. Rub the whole necklace with a polishing cloth to restore the finish on the chain, or use a tumbler with mixed stainless steel shot. Tumble the necklace for up to an hour (less if your beads are delicate).

safety tip
Never polish a chain with a motorized tool without proper training. Any loose material, such as cord or chain, can wrap around a power tool, possibly breaking your jewelry or injuring you. Hold all loose material inside your fist, exposing only one link at a time. Take the tool away or turn it off whenever you change position on the chain.

Soldered Charms

Design and make your own custom charms with sheet metal, shears, and stamps! Learn how to sweat-solder multiple layers of sheet metal and attach jump rings while making one of these simple calavera charms.

■ **techniques**
Sweat-soldering sheet metal
Cutting metal with shears
Stamping
Punching holes

■ **materials**
2x2 in. (51x51mm) 24-gauge sterling sheet
18-gauge copper sheet scrap
2 6mm OD 18-gauge sterling jump rings
Easy sterling solder
Rubber cement

■ **tools**
All tool sets plus steel design
    stamps, dividers
Micro butane torch

STEP 1: TRANSFER AND CUT OUT DESIGN

These instructions and this pattern are for making the calavera shown on the right on p. 64. Adapt the pattern to add a hat and a copper flower—or design your own charm!

Design a small charm, about ¾ in. (19mm) square (or just photocopy this pattern). Sketch the entire charm on paper, then make another drawing that shows two separate parts for the skull top and mouth **[A]**. Cut out the charm parts with scissors and glue them to a piece of 24-gauge sterling sheet with rubber cement. Let the glue dry for 5 minutes and rub off any excess. Trim around the parts with a pair of French shears **[B]**. (Sometimes it's easier to cut a small rectangle from the rest of the metal and then trim as close to the lines as possible.) Don't cut into the lines! You'll need them for the next step.

STEP 2: PUNCH HOLES AND FILE

Use a two-hole metal punch to make holes for the eyes. Use the large screw for one eye, and the small screw for the other **[C]**. Refine the shape of the charm with filing. Brace the charm on a V-slot bench pin and file away the excess metal with a medium-cut file, stopping at the lines on the paper **[D]**. For the nose, use a triangular needle file to make a crisp incision.

STEP 3: STAMP A DESIGN

You may want to practice stamping first on some scrap metal before you stamp your charm. Remove the paper from the charm and rub off any glue. Place the skull top face up on a steel block. Use an assortment of stamps to punch a pattern around the eyes. Use a thin, straight-line stamp to stamp the teeth **[E]**. Hold the stamp with your nondominant hand, with the design flat against the metal. Steady it while you strike the other end once with an unpolished hammer. Hitting steel with a polished hammer will nick the polished finish! Flatten the pieces on a bench block with a rawhide mallet after all the stamping is done **[F]**.

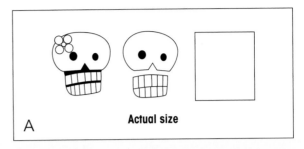

A

Actual size

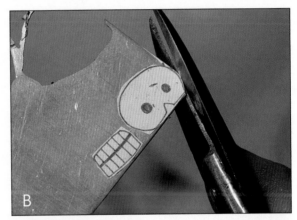

B

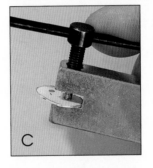

C

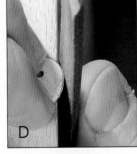

D

E

F

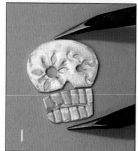

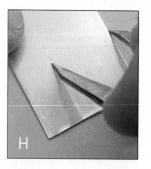

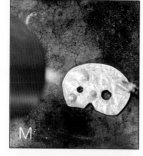

STEP 4: TRIM METAL FOR THE BACKGROUND

The charm will be mounted on a background piece of 24-gauge sterling, which should be just a little larger than the charm. Put the two pieces of the skull charm together. Turn the locking nut on a pair of *dividers* until the points are open a little wider than the widest point of the charm **[G]**. Drag one point of the dividers along the straight edge of the backing piece while scribing a parallel line with the other point **[H]**. Open the dividers a bit more than the height of the charm **[I]**. Scribe a second line at a right angle, moving the divider along the bottom edge of the metal **[J]**. Cut along the scribed lines with shears **[K]**. Flatten the piece with a mallet.

STEP 5: SWEAT-SOLDER THE SKULL TO THE BACKGROUND

Flux all sides of the charm pieces and place them face down on the solder board. Cut about four triple-length pieces of easy solder. Warm the flux until it turns clear with a neutral flame. Using tweezers, place the solder on the back of the skull top **[L]**. Switch to the solder pick and heat the solder until it melts, then use the pick to spread the molten solder evenly over the surface **[M]**. Don't use too much solder! A thin plating of solder that covers most of the surface is fine. Repeat these steps for the mouth piece.

Place the fluxed backing metal on the charcoal block. Pick up the skull top with tweezers and place it face up on the background. Switch to the solder pick and heat the pieces evenly with a neutral flame until they glow pink and molten solder runs out around the edges of the top layer **[N]**. The top piece can shift while soldering, so keep your pick ready to move it back into place. Working on a larger backing piece gives you a better margin for errors.

Repeat to sweat-solder the mouth to the backing **[O]**. Be conscious of any black scales of fire stain on the silver from the second soldering. Firescale develops easily during the intense heat of sweat-soldering, but the pickle and a little polishing will remove it. For now, quench, pickle, and rinse the charm. Check the edges to make sure the join filled completely. If lines still appear, mallet down any gaps, and then sweat-solder again by adding solder to the edge of the charm near the gaps.

STEP 6: TRIM AND FILE THE CHARM

Cut around the skull with shears **[P]**, cutting as close to the edge as possible without nicking it **[Q]**. Put the charm on the bench pin and file with the flat side of a large half-round or needle file to remove the rest of the excess metal **[R]**. To smooth the edges, hold the charm in a ring clamp while you file **[S]**.

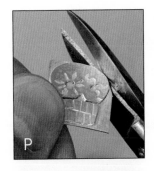 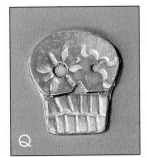

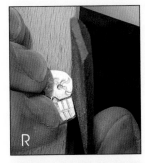 

STEP 7: SWEAT-SOLDER A FLOWER DESIGN TO THE CHARM

The metal screw punch is actually a very small disk cutter. When you punch a hole, a small dot of metal falls out. These dots are great for soldering patterns such as a flower onto the skull. If the dot gets stuck in the punch, just turn the handle to push it out.

For the petals, use the large screw to make four dots of 24-gauge sterling from your scrap sheet metal. For the center, use the small screw to make a dot from 18-gauge copper.

On the bench block, hammer ½ in. (13mm) of easy sterling solder wire until it is flat and thin. Cut and flux four small chips for the silver dots and one very small chip for the little copper dot. Flux the dots on both sides and place them on the solder board. Melt a chip of easy solder to the back of each dot **[T]**.

Flux both sides of the skull and place it on the charcoal block. Glaze the flux with a neutral flame. Use tweezers to flip the dots over and arrange them on the skull as shown while it's warm. Switch to the solder pick. Heat the entire charm evenly until the dots sweat-solder to the charm **[U]**. As the charm heats up, the flux can move the dots around, so keep them in place with the pick. If the dots solder in the wrong place, hold the charm down with a third hand, heat the charm, and then slide the dot back in place with the pick when the solder is molten again. Quench, pickle, and rinse the charm.

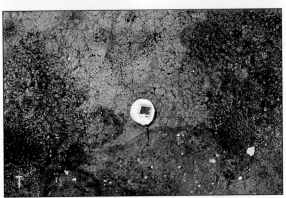

STEP 8: SWEAT-SOLDER A JUMP RING TO THE CHARM

Working on the solder board, solder closed a 6mm 18-gauge sterling jump ring. Add a second piece of easy solder on top of the join and let it melt only partially, leaving a lump on the ring **[V]**. This tall lump will make it obvious when the solder flows and the charm drops onto the jump ring.

Move the jump ring onto the charcoal block. Place the fluxed charm face up on top, with the join and solder lump centered under it near the top of the skull. Position the block so you can see the gap between the charm and ring **[W]**. Heat only the charm until it glows pink; it will fall into place on the jump ring when the solder flows **[X]**. Quench.

STEP 9: ADD A SECOND JUMP RING

Before pickling, attach a second jump ring. Close the jump ring for soldering. Using a third hand, hold it by the jump ring soldered to the charm as shown. Flux the new jump ring and the charm, and close it with easy solder **[Y]**. Quench, pickle for 20 minutes or longer, and rinse. Clean up the edges and remove any traces of the seams with silicone polishing wheels. Polish the rest of the charm with radial disks, starting with 120- or 220-grit radials to strip off any firescale.

Mixed-Metals Pendant

Watching your first seam flow in a fluid quicksilver streak is thrilling. Tiny pieces of solder can flow such a long way! In this project, you'll practice soldering seams, learn how to use a soldering tripod, and make a custom bail for your mixed-metals pendant.

techniques
Soldering seams
Dapping
Making and attaching a bail
Using a soldering tripod

tools
All tool sets plus wood dapping
   block and punch, border
   design stamps
Jumbo butane torch

materials
24-gauge sterling disk, ⅞ in. (22mm) diameter
18-gauge copper disk, 1 in. (25.5mm) diameter
24-gauge sterling sheet scrap, at least 1x1 in.
6mm OD 18-gauge sterling jump ring
Easy sterling solder
Masking or painter's tape

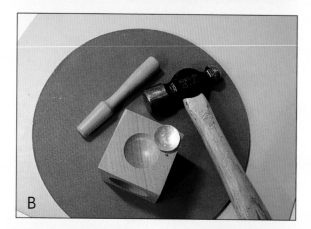

A

B

C

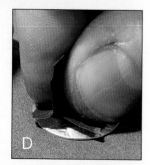

D

E

F

STEP 1: TEXTURE THE DISKS

Use the wedge end of a polished cross-peen hammer to texture the copper and one of the sterling disks. (The patterned copper will be the back of the pendant.) Turn the disk randomly as you hammer to create a pattern **[A]**.

Texture is fun to create and it reduces polishing time, since it disguises the flaws that stand out on a flat, bare surface.

STEP 2: DAP THE STERLING DISK

To dome the silver disk for the pendant and preserve its texture, use a wood dapping block and punch set with an unpolished household hammer **[B]**. To make a shallow dome, use a depression that is half again larger than the diameter of the disk. Place the disk texture side down in the center. The wood dapping set pictured comes with a one-size-daps-all punch. The domed sterling disk will end up noticeably smaller than the copper disk **[C]**, which will leave enough space to stamp a border in the copper later.

STEP 3: SAND THE EDGES AND PUNCH A HOLE

Sand the bottom edge of the dome to make it perfectly flat: Use 320-grit sandpaper and work on a flat, clean surface such as your tabletop. Make a little handle with tape (masking or painter's tape works well) to hold the metal **[D]**. Change direction often as you sand. Check the fit against the copper disk; you should see no gaps in the seam **[E]** as there were earlier **[C]**. Punch a small hole near the top of the copper disk **[F]** so air can escape during soldering.

It's very important to leave holes for air and steam to escape whenever soldering hollow objects. Objects like this pendant and the beads and boxes constructed in later projects can explode if there is no escape valve.

STEP 4: SOLDER THE DISKS TOGETHER

Cut 8–10 double-length pieces of easy solder wire and flux them. Completely flux both disks. Note that oil and dirt on the metal can repel the water-based flux, leaving metal exposed to firescale when it's heated **[G]**. Apply the flux to *warm* metal and it will fill the gaps.

Cleaning the metal with pumice or alcohol, pickling, sanding, or scrubbing may help hold the flux in place, but often the flux will still pull away. Warming the metal before applying flux will solve this.

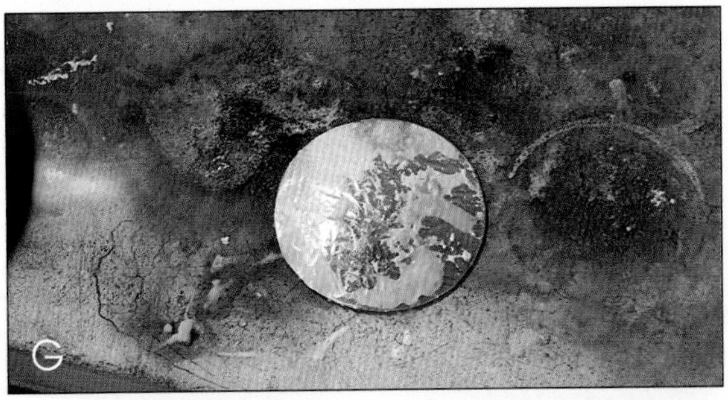

G

Start with the domed top side of the silver disk. Dab a little wet flux on the bare metal and warm the metal lightly to around 200°F (93°C). At this low temperature, the flux will sizzle as the water boils away, leaving a coat of white, powdery borax behind. Continue to keep the metal warm, moving the flame away as you dab more flux on any gaps with the brush **[H]**. Don't overdo it! Too much flux will interfere with soldering. Later, when the flux clears at 1100°F (593°C), it will spread out and fill any tiny gaps. What you want at this stage is an even, light coat of flux **[I]**. Repeat to coat the inside of the dome and both sides of the copper disk.

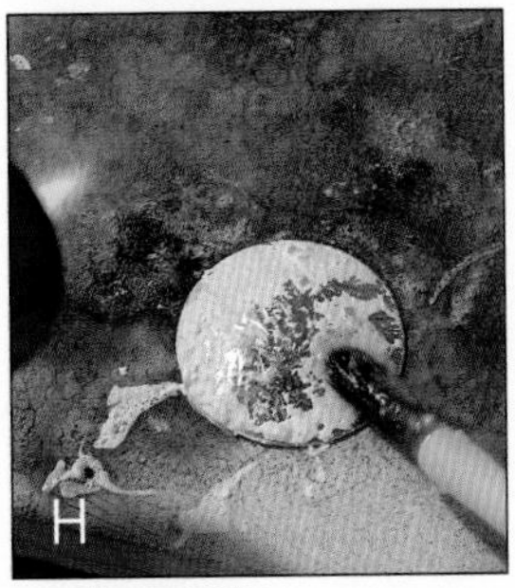

H

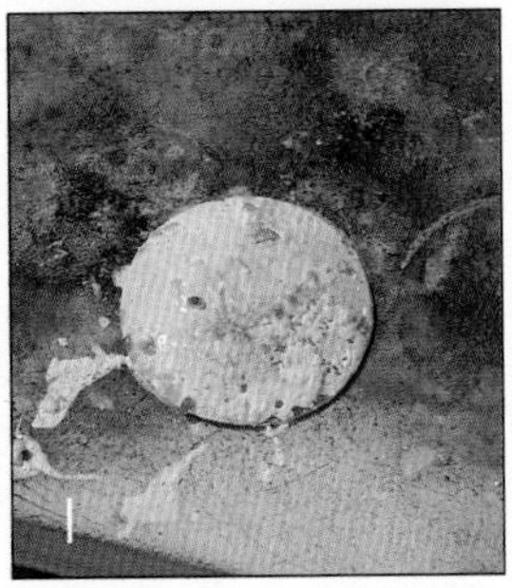

I

Set up a soldering tripod to heat the metal from underneath, which will help to keep the solder from crawling up onto the dome before it flows around the seam. The tripod should be on the ceramic tile, to the side of your solder board. You will use the torch upside down with the flame under the mesh during soldering. Use the jumbo butane torch, because a small torch may not be able to heat both the mesh and the disks.

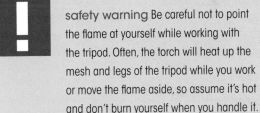

> **!** safety warning Be careful not to point the flame at yourself while working with the tripod. Often, the torch will heat up the mesh and legs of the tripod while you work or move the flame aside, so assume it's hot and don't burn yourself when you handle it.

Using tweezers, place the copper disk texture side down in the center of the mesh. Warm the copper from underneath until the flux turns clear. As it clears, move the flame aside and use tweezers to center the sterling dome on the copper. Bring the flame back under the copper to keep it warm as you nudge the dome into position with the pick **[J]**.

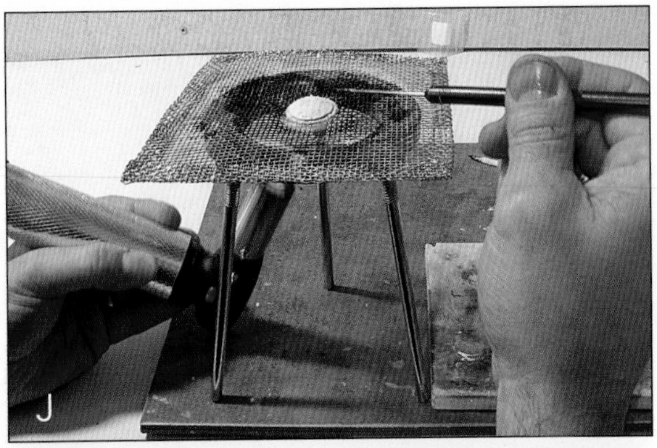

J

Be careful to take the flame on and off the metal to hold this lower temperature while you work. The steel mesh will continue to heat the metal after you take the flame away, so remove the heat a little earlier than usual.

Continue to simmer the metal, holding the temperature at a point where the metal looks matte and clean and the flux is clear. Use tweezers to place the 8–10 chips of easy solder spaced evenly around the dome where it meets the copper disk, flush to the seam. Increase the fuel for more heat and place the tip of the cone inside the flame, just underneath the copper. The steel mesh should glow brightly under the metal **[K]**. Keep the heat inside the border of the copper disk and

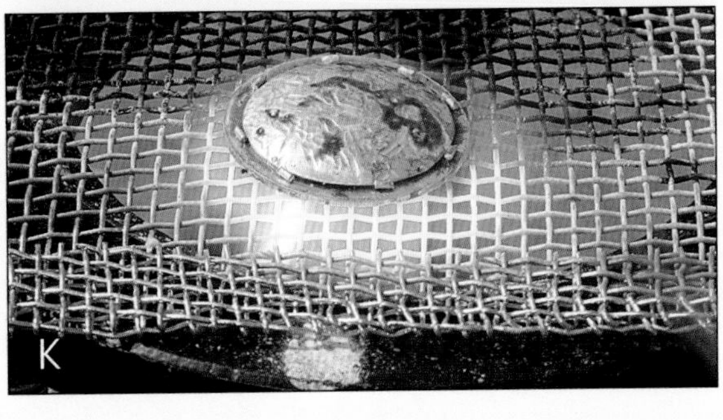

K

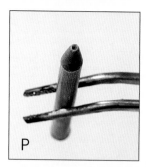

move slowly. As the solder starts to flow, it will melt down and then into the seam. Continue heating until the silver glows pale pink and the solder flows completely around the seam **[L]**. Use tweezers to turn the mesh by the corners as you work so you can check all sides of the piece. Remove the heat. Quench the piece, pickle for 5 minutes, and rinse.

To fix any gaps in the seam, first try to close any big holes with a mallet and steel block. Place the pendant with the flat side down on the steel and tap the edge of the silver over the gap with a mallet, being careful not to smash the dome. Then place fresh solder on any gaps and solder them closed.

STEP 5: STAMP A BORDER DESIGN AND FILE

After pickling, solder stains will probably be visible, especially on the copper **[M]**. Polish them away with 220-grit radial disks **[N]**. Be careful not to remove any texture or distort the thickness of the copper.

Practice stamping on scrap metal to warm up and make sure you like the design before you stamp the pendant.

Stamp the border with a pattern. The first stamp used to make the half-circle pattern is a large nail set with a cupped end **[O]**. A second, smaller stamp with a cupped end is used between each of the half-circles **[P]**. The combination of two simple shapes makes a great border design **[Q]**.

STEP 6: SWEAT-SOLDER A JUMP RING TO THE BORDER

Use the same steps outlined in the soldered charms project (step 8) to add a 6mm OD 18-gauge sterling jump ring to the back of the pendant. Make a line with a permanent marker on the front of the pendant where the jump ring should be centered. Solder the jump ring closed with easy solder. Add another chip of solder and tack it in place on the back. Apply the flux to the warm pendant for an even coat, as described in step 4 above. Position the fluxed jump ring and pendant on the charcoal block, centering the ring on the line. Heat mostly the pendant; aim the flame sideways across the middle, with a slow, even flame until the solder flows and it drops down to the ring **[R]**. Don't overheat the jump ring or you'll get a false drop when the solder flows only onto the ring. Quench, pickle for 5 minutes, and rinse. Check to make sure the ring is securely soldered before continuing.

STEP 7: MAKE AND ATTACH A BAIL

Stamp a piece of 24-gauge sterling sheet with a complementary pattern across an area approximately ¼×1 in. (6.5x25mm) **[S]**. Using a marker, draw a narrow oval with two sharply tapered ends. Cut out the shape with French shears **[T]**. Refine the shape with files. Place the midpoint at the base of the roundnose pliers. To form a bail, fold the ends with your finger, keeping the textured side out **[U]**. Hold the bail in a ring clamp and use the flat side of a medium-cut file to make the sides even. Check the results as you file and make sure the bail is symmetrical **[V]**. Open the clamp, flip the bail over, and repeat on the other side.

Remove any file marks and make a flat plane from wide top to narrow bottom by sanding each side on 320-grit sandpaper **[W]**. Open the bail by inserting chainnose pliers inside the loop and opening the pliers **[X]**. Insert the bail into the jump ring attached to the pendant. Use chainnose pliers to close the bail **[Y]**. The bail should fit far enough into the jump ring that the join can point up and away from the pendant. If not, file the bail to make it narrow enough to fit.

Flux the pendant and bail. Heat only the bail and warm it to apply a ball of easy solder to the join **[Z]**. Move the flame up and down the sides of the bail, then focus on the join. Repeat until it's soldered. Quench, pickle for 20 minutes or longer, and rinse. Shake out any water onto a towel, or allow the piece to air-dry completely before finishing. (Water has a nasty habit of mixing with polishing dust to make a nice, gooey paste.)

STEP 8: FINISHING

Polish the pendant with radial disks to avoid wearing away the texture. Position the wheels so the bristles are in line with the texture. Start with 220-grit radials to remove any firescale and excess solder. Spot-finish any stubborn scratches with silicone polishing wheels, finishing with blue (fine) grit and blending the surface with the radial disks. You can use pin polishers to clean up the inside of the bail, if desired. Accent the pattern on the border and the bail with a liver-of-sulfur patina. To avoid darkening the whole pendant, apply the patina with a cotton swab to just the border and bail. As soon as these areas get dark, neutralize the piece in water and baking soda. Remove excess patina from the highlights with a polishing pad or another round of extra-fine-grit polishing. Use a wheel that will stay out of the recesses without leaving a lot of residue to clean up, such as a pink silicone polishing wheel.

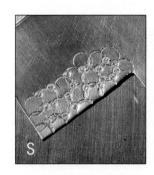
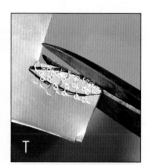
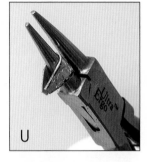

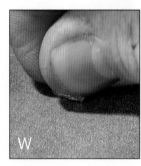
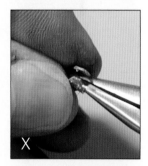
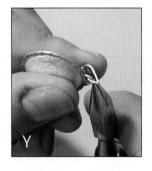

Textured Ring with Borders

This textured, flared ring changes size as hammering and shaping stretches the metal. Measuring the ring blank, sizing, and forming are all basic skills for making a ring.

techniques
Forming a ring
Soldering a ring
Resizing rings
Adding matching borders

tools
All tool sets plus tapered steel ring mandrel, dividers, steel dapping punch
Jumbo butane torch

materials
1x3 in. (25.5x76mm) 20-gauge sterling sheet
12 in. (30.5cm) 16-gauge sterling round wire
Easy sterling solder
Medium sterling solder

STEP 1: MEASURE THE RING BLANK

Using a ring mandrel, determine the size of a ring that fits you comfortably, or use a set of finger gauges. (See "Measuring Your Ring Size" on p. 106 for more details.)

This ring will be textured with flared sides; it will stretch and grow as you shape it, so the size of the blank has to be adjusted. For example, after making a prototype of this ring, I found that the ring stretched about 3.5 sizes by the time it was done! So, to make a size 8.5 ring, I started with a size 5 ring blank. If you want to skip the flaring, size the blank two sizes smaller and texture until the ring is the right size in step 5.

Subtract 3.5 from your ring size and, looking at the column for 20-gauge metal on the Ring Blank Size by Metal Gauge table on p. 108, find the starting length in millimeters. Mark that length on the sterling sheet. Set a pair of dividers to 5mm and drag one point along the edge of the metal as you scribe a parallel line **[A]**. Cut out the blank with French shears. Each end should be straight and perpendicular to the length. Using a rawhide mallet, flatten the blank on a steel block **[B]**. If the strip warps or curves, place it on its edge, with the concave edge facing the steel block, and tap gently on the opposite edge to straighten it.

STEP 2: FORM THE CENTER BAND

You'll shape the band on a ring mandrel with a rawhide mallet, first curving both ends of the blank. Work on the ring mandrel at the size that matches the starting point for the ring—in this case, size 5. Rest one end of the mandrel on a pad, such as a towel, on the edge of the table. Place the blank on the mandrel, with one end extending ½ in. (13mm) **[C]**. Hit the end with the mallet, curving it against the mandrel **[D]**. Repeat on the other end of the blank, curving the metal in the same direction. Extend the blank another ½ in. **[E]** and hit it again with the mallet. Continue to curve and extend the blank until it's wrapped around the mandrel **[F]**. Squeeze it closed to check the size. It should be close to your starting size. If the size is larger or more than a half-size smaller than your size, check the measurement against the ring blank size chart. If it's too large, trim it to size. If it's a half-size smaller, you can resize it after soldering (see p. 107).

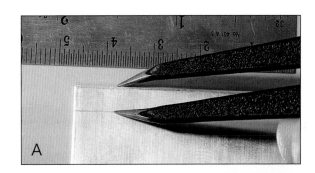

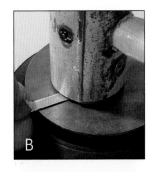

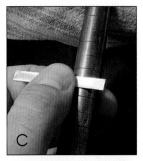

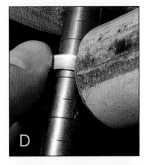

STEP 3: CLOSE THE JOIN FOR SOLDERING

After forming, the seam has to be flush from top to bottom for it to solder and to disappear after texturing and polishing. Use a pair of half-round pliers to close the join: Place the half-round jaw inside the curve and the flat jaw on the outside **[G]**. Hold one side of the join and pivot the pliers to move the metal toward the other end. Repeat on the other end. Don't squeeze too hard or you might crush the metal and round the middle of the join.

It's OK if you flatten the band at the join, creating a letter D in order to close the seam. You can reshape the band after you solder it.

Close the seam with tension by overlapping the ends. First, overlap one end over the other **[H]**. Then reverse it to overlap that end under **[I]**. Bring the seam together and check the fit. Even a slight gap in the band won't solder completely, or could break open during the rest of the forming; photo **[J]** shows a tiny gap near the top of the seam that needs to be corrected before soldering.

File the join with a straight, flat needle file **[K]**. Open the band slightly wider than the file and hold the band with the flat end of a ring clamp. The join should be just above the clamp. File one side at a time, using the other side as a guide to help keep them parallel. Rest the bottom edge of the file against the ring clamp as you file forward with short strokes; long strokes can curve slightly, rounding the corners of the seam and leaving more gaps. After a few file strokes, reverse the ring clamp and file the other side of the seam. Check the join again by repeating the steps above until the seam is perfectly flush **[L]**.

STEP 4: SOLDER THE BAND

Cut two small chips of medium solder, place them on the solder board, and flux them. Flux the entire band, inside and out, and place it on the charcoal block. Warm it with the jumbo butane torch and fill in any gaps in the flux.

Scoop up a ball of medium solder with the pick and warm the entire band until the flux turns clear. As it clears, keep it warm with the torch, then stick the solder to the top of the join **[M]**. Warm the back of the band and center the heat on the join, repeating this slow movement until the solder flows. Look for bright, light red rather than pink as a sign that the metal is hot enough to melt the medium solder. Using medium solder for this join will keep it from opening when the borders are attached later with lower-temperature easy solder.

Quench, pickle, and rinse the band. Examine the join. The band should be completely soldered, inside **[N]** and out **[O]**, from corner to corner. If it's not, flux and solder the ring again.

STEP 5: RESHAPE, TEXTURE, AND SAND THE BAND

Dry the ring completely. Place it on the ring mandrel again, and tap it with the mallet, moving all around the ring to reshape it **[P]**. Reverse the ring on the mandrel and do this step again. The ring should be the right starting size now—in this case, size 5. If it's up to a half-size larger or smaller, you should be able to compensate while you're increasing the size with texturing.

Use a polished cross-peen hammer to texture the ring on the mandrel **[Q]**. Be careful to hammer evenly or it will curve and distort. As the ring grows, pull it down the mandrel, keeping it snug against the steel. After completing one course around, reverse the ring on the mandrel and repeat. Stop after the ring is completely textured. The size will grow again after flaring the sides in the next step.

Remove the ring from the mandrel and place it on the steel block; tap it with the mallet to straighten it **[R]**. Don't let the band twist. Because bumps or dirt on the work surface will distort the sanding, clean the surface before placing a piece of 220-grit wet/dry sandpaper for metal on a clean, flat tabletop. Sand the edges of the ring so that the band is even and parallel **[S]**. Keep the sandpaper flat on the table with one hand. Reverse the band and sand the other side. The edges should be flat on both sides.

STEP 6: FLARE THE SIDES OF THE RING

For an interesting design, flare the edges of the ring slightly with a steel dapping punch on the steel block **[T]**. Use a punch that is larger than the ring and won't touch the block when it's inside the band. Center the punch inside the ring and hit the other end with an unpolished 8 oz. ball-peen hammer. The top should start to curve outward. Reverse the ring and repeat. Be careful not to twist the band with too much hammering. Mallet the ring on the steel block to straighten the sides if need be. Sand the edges flat again.

Check the size of the ring on the mandrel again. It should be the final size before going on to the next step. If not, you will have to size it (see p. 107). Since the ring is now curved, stretching with even a rawhide mallet could twist it if you're not careful. It might actually be easier to cut the ring open and add or remove metal to properly size it.

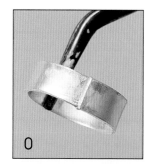

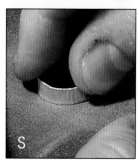

STEP 7: MAKE MATCHING BORDERS

Use the Ring Blank Size by Metal Gauge table to find the length for the 16-gauge wire borders. Use the 16-gauge column and match the size to the final size of the ring. Flush-cut one end of the wire, measure, and cut the other end flush, too. Repeat for a second length of wire.

Repeat steps 3 and 4 to form and solder the rings closed with medium solder. Quench, pickle, and rinse. Dry the border rings and reshape them to size on the mandrel with the rawhide mallet. Flatten the rings on the steel block. Sand one side of each border ring flat for easier soldering to the center band [U]. Check the fit of the borders with the top and bottom of the center band. If necessary, stretch a border ring on the mandrel by lightly tapping it downward toward the thick end of the mandrel [V].

STEP 8: SWEAT-SOLDER THE BORDERS TO THE BAND

Flatten 1 in. (25.5mm) of easy solder wire. Cut and flux 16–18 small chips and place them on the solder board. Flux the center band inside and out and place it next to the board. Flux one of the border rings and place it flat side up on the solder board. Heat the border until the flux stops bubbling and turns clear. Move the heat aside, but keep the ring warm as you place eight chips of easy solder on the flat edge [W], spacing them evenly. Continue to heat the border ring until the solder melts flat to the metal.

Move the border ring to the charcoal block. Place the center band on top of the ring and center it [X]. Heat the band from the inside and bring the temperature up on both parts evenly. As the band starts to glow light pink, bring the heat to the outside and heat around the sides [Y]. A visible seam of molten solder should flow between the pieces. Stand by with the pick in case the rings shift during soldering. Don't overheat the rings or you might open the join on the band.

Repeat to solder the second border ring to the band [Z]. Quench, pickle for 20 minutes or longer, and rinse. Check the ring size one more time and make any adjustments if necessary.

STEP 9: FINISHING

Remove any excess solder and defects with silicone polishing wheels. Use radial disks to continue polishing, starting with 220-grit radials to remove any firescale. Turn the wheels so the bristles are aligned with the texture to preserve it. Use small wheels to polish inside the ring.

Squashed Beads

Making round metal beads is classic soldering practice, but so ordinary. For a twist, why not completely change their shape with a hammer? Get a bonus lesson in this project: a clever trick for making a custom tool to hold the two bead halves together for soldering.

█ techniques	█ tools
Soldering a hollow bead	All tool sets plus dapping
Forming metal on "air"	block and punches
	Extra pair of cross-locking
	tweezers
	Jumbo butane torch

█ materials

2 24-gauge ⅞ in. (22mm) diameter sterling disks
4 24-gauge ¾ in. (19mm) diameter sterling disks
Easy sterling solder

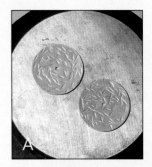

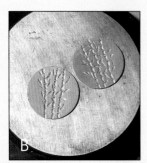

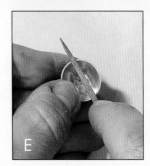

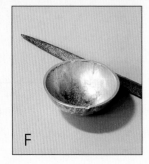

STEP 1: STAMP, DAP, AND SAND THE DISKS

Hammer a pattern on one side of each of the large disks **[A]**. For the smaller disks, you can use the same pattern or stamp a complementary design **[B]**.

Use a steel dapping set to dome the disks into matching pairs for the beads **[C]**. Make the domes as round and deep as possible. Sand the edge of each dome flat with 320-grit sandpaper **[D]**. (Make sure the table is clean under the paper; any bumps can wobble the edge of the dome and make it harder to solder the seam.)

STEP 2: FILE NOTCHES FOR DRILLING LATER

To allow air to escape during soldering and to make it easier to drill the beads later, notch the edges of one half of each bead pair with a triangular needle file. Make a notch on one side **[E]**. Then, mark the opposite side of the bead, dividing it perfectly in half. Notch the second side **[F]**. Notching only half of the bead avoids any problems with misalignment during soldering and keeps the holes lined up for drilling later. Don't make the notches too shallow or they might fill with solder.

STEP 3: MAKE A CUSTOM TOOL TO HOLD THE BEADS FOR SOLDERING

It's challenging to try to line up two domes to solder and make a bead. I recommend customizing a pair of cross-locking tweezers into a bead-holding tool by bending the ends. The best tweezers for this job have fiberboard handles to insulate your fingers from the heat. You have to anneal the steel to make it soft enough to bend, but that's easy enough. If you make all the beads similar in shape, one set of curved tweezers should work for all of them.

Heat 1 in. (25.5mm) of the tweezers' tips until they glow red and hold that color for 30 seconds **[G]**. Let the steel cool slowly—don't quench! When it's cold, use a pair of half-round pliers to bend the tips outward almost 90 degrees, then curve them to match your beads **[H]**. Test the fit on the unfluxed beads and make any adjustments before soldering. Be sure that the tweezer tips are not pinching the beads or you'll dent them when the silver is red hot and soft.

STEP 4: SOLDER THE BEADS

Flatten 1½ in. (38mm) of easy solder wire with a hammer and steel block; cut and flux about 24 chips. Place the domed bead halves on the solder board and flux all sides, applying the flux while you apply a little heat on the metal to completely cover the surfaces. Choose one pair, and heat one side. When the flux turns clear, simmer the heat on and off to keep the flux tacky while you evenly spread eight chips of solder along the flat edge with tweezers **[I]**. After placing each chip, warm it slightly to let it sink into the liquid flux. Too little heat, and the chips will fall off. Too much heat and they may slide into the center or melt too soon.

After the solder is in place, move the bead to a cool spot on the board and let it cool for 1–2 minutes, until it's safe to touch. The flux should be hard enough to glue the solder in place. Gently put the two halves of the bead together and hold them with the modified tweezers **[J]**.

Hold the tweezers in your dominant hand and heat the bead with the torch. Rotate the tweezers to turn the bead so it heats evenly on all sides. As the silver gets close to the right temperature, it will glow light pink to red and the seam will close as the solder flows **[K]**. The last part to close is the seam between the jaws of the tweezers, where the cold steel slows down the heat. Be sure to direct some heat along the seam there. If you need a free hand to add solder, use the pick, and so on, lay the tweezers on your solder board or prop them against the charcoal block.

Solder the remaining bead pairs. Quench carefully in water, pickle for 5–10 minutes, and rinse. Check the seams for gaps before going on to the next step, because the join has to be strong enough to take the stress of hammering.

The bead will probably be full of water and pickle. If the notches haven't filled with solder, you can heat the bead lightly (to about 200°F/93°C) on the solder board to evaporate any water. Watch out for jets of water! Immediately dry off any steel tools that get wet. Make sure the beads are completely dry inside and out before proceeding.

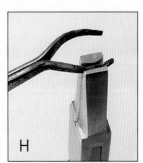

81

STEP 5: DRILL THE BEADS AND FILE THE SEAMS

Hold a bead in the ring clamp. Support the bead on a block of wood and open the notch into a hole with a 1/16-in. (1.6mm) or smaller drill bit [L]. Reverse the bead in the clamp and drill the opposite side. Hold the bead with a ring clamp or support it on a bench pin as you smooth the seam using the flat side of a medium-cut file [M]. Repeat for the remaining two beads.

STEP 6: ALTER THE BEAD SHAPES

If the seams are strong, the beads can be hammered into other shapes. Domes and spheres have a lot of structural strength, and it takes a lot of force to break them open.

Rest the large bead on a steel block with one hole at the top. Use the flat side of a polished hammer to flatten the sides [N, O]. Keep the hole in the center of the depression. The opposite side will flatten at the same time against the steel block; flip the bead over and repeat this step on the other side to even it out. Repeat for the two smaller beads.

To give the large bead a squarish cushion shape, turn the bead along the seam and center it between the two flat sides just hammered. Use the same hammer face to flatten the top and bottom [P]. To curve the sides in a little more, switch to the round end of a polished ball peen and hammer each side again [Q].

STEP 7: FINISHING

Remove file marks on the seams with silicone wheels, black (medium) through blue (fine). Polish the rest of the bead with radial disks, starting with 220-grit to remove any firescale. Be careful not to remove your stamping and texture. Add patina if desired and polish the highlights to bring out the texture.

TROUBLESHOOTING

If the hole moves out of position during hammering, you can plug it up and drill it again. Find a gauge of sterling wire thick enough to plug the hole and taper the end with files. Flux the bead and wedge the wire tightly in the hole. Solder it with easy solder. Cut the wire with flush-cutters and file or grind the nub off with polishing wheels. Use a 2mm steel ball bur to grind a depression for the drill bit in the new, correct location. Hold the bead as described before and drill the hole again. **If the seam opens during hammering,** stop and mallet the edges back together, and solder the bead again.

Box Clasp

A box clasp is a simple
mechanism, yet it's a stylish
custom-made addition
for a bracelet or necklace
that communicates the
high quality of your work. A
folded tab, called a tongue,
locks inside a keyhole cut
into the side of the box.

techniques
Fabricating a small box
Making and adjusting a clasp
Soldering seams

tools
All tool sets plus tapered steel
   ring mandrel, dividers
Jumbo butane torch

materials
3x4 in. (7.6x10.2cm) 24 or 26-gauge patterned
   sterling sheet
2x3 in. (51x76mm) 24-gauge sterling sheet
2 6mm OD 18-gauge sterling jump rings
Easy sterling solder
Medium sterling solder

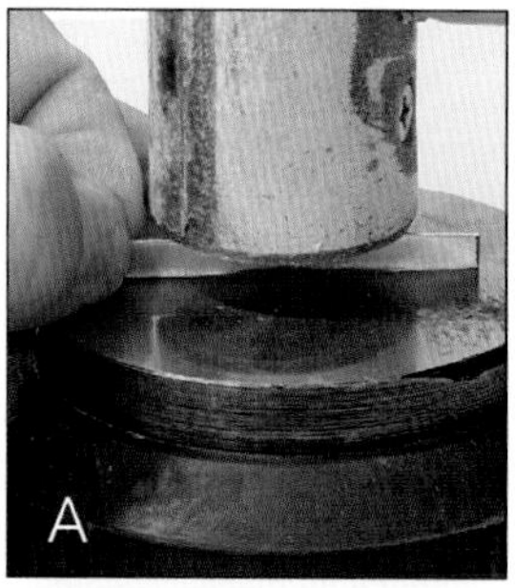
A

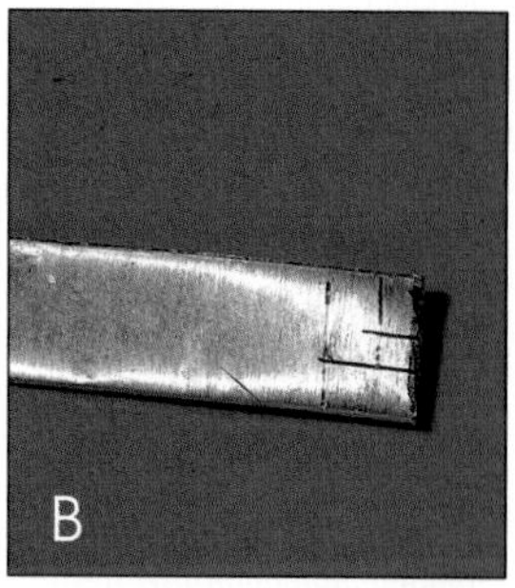
B

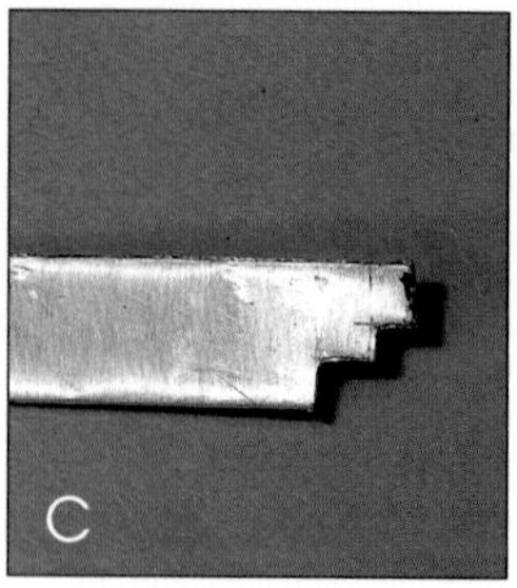
C

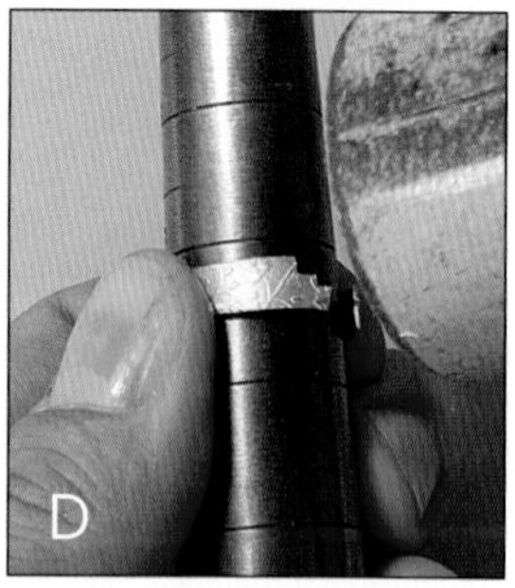
D

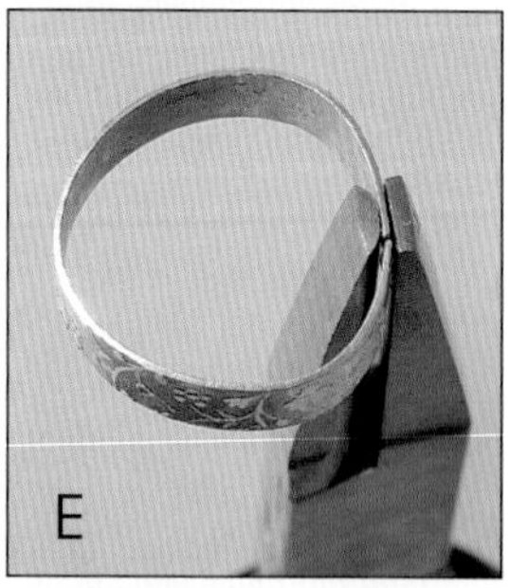
E

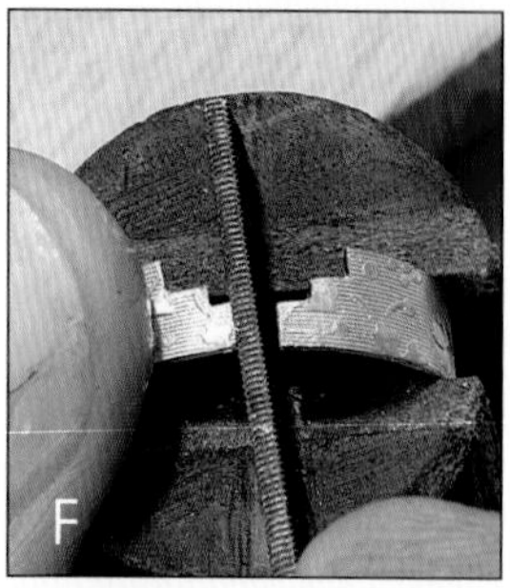
F

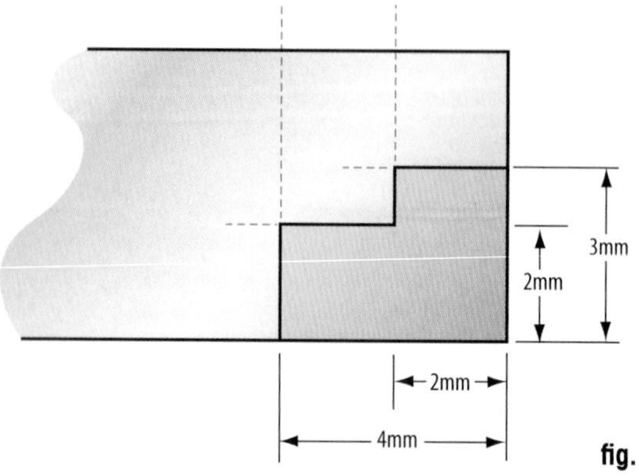
3mm
2mm
2mm
4mm

fig. 1

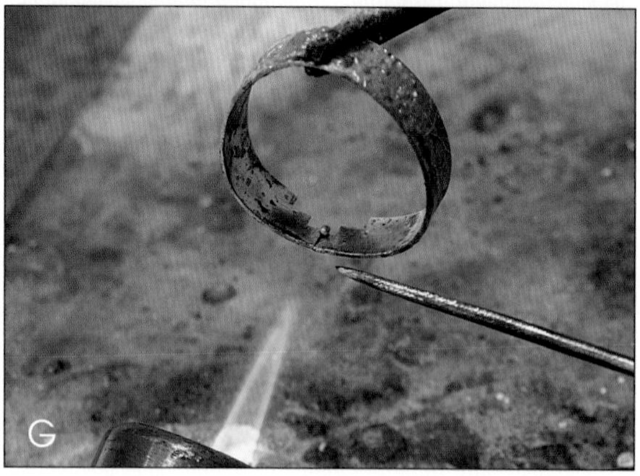
G

The process for making a box bead is similar to making this clasp: Simply skip the keyhole and punch two holes in the sides before you solder on the top and the base. I've also included notes for making a square or oval box.

STEP 1: SHAPE THE BOX WALL AND KEYHOLE

Start by measuring and cutting a strip of 24-gauge patterned sterling sheet to make the ring-shaped wall of the box. Set a pair of dividers to 5mm for the height and scribe a parallel line. For a round box, the length is equal to π (3.14) multiplied by the diameter of the clasp. For example, for a 25mm diameter box, the length would be 25mm x 3.14 = 78.5mm. (For a square, add up the lengths of each side to get the length of the strip.) Trim the strip to size with French shears, making sure that each end is cut at a right angle.

Sometimes the metal will be curved after shearing. Place it on a steel block, with the curved edge facing down, and gently tap with a mallet along the edge to straighten it **[A]**. File the strip to smooth, if necessary.

Next you'll cut half of the keyhole into each end of the strip. (To make a simple box bead instead, skip this step and make two holes after soldering and reshaping the strip in step 2.) Working on the back of the patterned sheet, use dividers to scribe guidelines **[fig. 1]**. Scribe a short line 2mm above the bottom edge. Open the dividers to 3mm and scribe a second line above the first. Change the dividers to 2mm and, using the join line as a guide, scribe a vertical line to make a small square in the upper right. Scribe a second vertical line at 4mm, which will make a bigger rectangle to the left of the small box **[B]**. Use shears to cut out half of the keyhole (the shaded area in the figure). Use a square needle file to refine the shape **[C]**. Repeat on the other end of the strip, flipping the reference figure on the vertical axis. The second keyhole must mirror the first, forming a symmetrical stepped pattern, so they align for soldering. Shape the strip on a ring mandrel with a mallet **[D]**. Close and align the join with half-round pliers **[E]**. If the seam has gaps, smooth with a flat needle file **[F]** using short, forward strokes.

STEP 2: SOLDER AND RESHAPE

Flux the inside and outside of the ring shape. Pick up the blank with tweezers and place it in a third hand, holding the metal on the opposite side from the join. Face the join toward the solder board. Arrange the space so that you can comfortably heat from underneath and inside the blank. Warm the ring lightly and fill in any gaps in the flux.

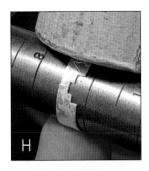

Cut and flux two small chips of medium sterling solder. Start by heating inside and under the top of the ring to warm the silver away from the join, then bring the torch down under the seam. Repeat until the flux turns clear, then place a ball of solder on the far side of the join **[G]**. Repeat the heating pattern, dwelling longer with each round under the seam until the solder flows. Placing the solder on the opposite end of the seam from the flame and heating it from underneath helps the solder to flow through the join. Make sure the join is filled, then quench, pickle for a few minutes, and rinse. Put the ring back on the mandrel and shape it with a mallet **[H]**. Reverse the ring and repeat once.

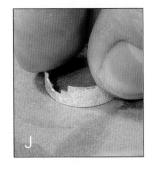

For an oval box, use an oval mandrel or stretch the ring into an oval by opening a pair of pliers inside it. For a square box, skip the ring mandrel and use a square mandrel or flat pliers to adjust the shape after soldering.

Use a flat or a barrette needle file to refine the shape of the keyhole before soldering on the top and base **[I]**. Sand the top and bottom edges flat on 320-grit sandpaper **[J]**. Remember to change direction often to avoid tapering the ring.

STEP 3: SOLDER THE RING TO THE BASE

Use the dividers to take a measurement a little bigger than the diameter of the ring **[K]**. (It's much easier to position the ring on a larger square blank for soldering, whether you'll add a border or not.) Scribe two squares on 24-gauge sterling sheet and trim them with shears.

Texture the top and base squares with hammers or stamps **[L]**. Flatten the squares with a mallet and bench block. Check the fit between the sides and the base for gaps **[M]**.

Cut and flux 8–10 double-length pieces of easy solder. Flux and place the base, texture side down, on a soldering tripod. Add the ring, also fluxed inside and out; place it in the center

of the base. Warm the sterling from underneath with the jumbo torch until the flux starts to turn clear. Remember: The hot steel will keep heating the silver even after you remove the flame. As the flux clears, the seam between the ring and the base will settle and close. Move the heat aside, but keep the piece warm while you place eight pieces of solder around the seam with tweezers **[N]**.

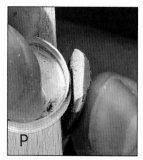

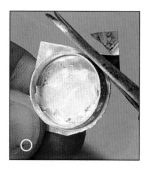

Place the chips inside the box to protect the pattern from being flooded with solder. Continue to heat from underneath until the silver starts to glow light pink to red and the flux clears even more. Increase the heat by bringing the flame over the sterling at the last minute to make the solder flow faster. Make sure the first join in the ring hasn't opened. Remove from heat, quench, pickle, and rinse.

Check the seam for gaps and repeat this step if you find any. Place the box upside down on a steel block, with the gap facing you. Gently tap on the base over the gap to close the seam and then solder again. Trim the excess silver from the base. For this design, leave enough to make a narrow border **[O]**. File the border to a consistent thickness **[P]**.

STEP 4: SOLDER THE TOP

Check the fit between the top and box. Make any adjustments, if necessary, with more flattening or sanding. Cut and flux 8–10 double-length chips of easy solder. Completely flux the top piece and place it on the tripod, texture side down. Flux the rest of the box, inside and out, and place it in the center of the top piece. Repeat to solder the seam, placing the chips of easy solder around the outside of the seam this time **[Q]**. Again, heating mostly from underneath will draw the solder down and around the seam, not up and over the patterned silver. Quench, pickle for 2 minutes, and rinse. Check the seams and fix any gaps before continuing. Shake out any water and dry the box.

Trim away the excess silver and file to match the base. When the two borders are close to the same size, file them at the same time to make them match **[R]**.

STEP 5: ADD A JUMP RING

Cut a 6mm OD 18-gauge sterling jump ring across its join, making a horseshoe shape **[S]**. Flux the box and place it on a charcoal block. Use a third hand to hold the jump ring level against the side of the box, opposite the keyhole and just above the border. Flux the jump ring. Heat mostly the box to clear the flux. Place one ball of easy solder on each end of the jump ring **[T]**. Keep the flame only on the box as you continue to heat it; too much heat on the jump ring and the solder will pull away from the joins.

Watch the solder as you work. If it starts to pull toward the box, move the flame quickly to the jump ring to pull it into the joins. Quench and pickle while you form the tongue.

STEP 6: FORM THE TONGUE FOR THE CLASP

The tongue is made from a folded piece of 24-gauge sterling sheet. It has to fit through the keyhole and snap up into the smaller section, locking the clasp against the wide shoulders of the tongue. A tab sticks out so it can be squeezed to release the catch and open the clasp. The bottom of the tongue has a jump ring or hole for attaching to one end of a necklace or bracelet.

The tongue should be as wide as the widest part of the keyhole, which is 8mm. Scribe a parallel line along the long edge of the plain sterling sheet. The length can vary considerably but should be less than twice the diameter of the box, plus 5–8mm for the tab. The jump ring will add length, too. It's better for the tongue to be a little short rather than too long—too long and it won't fit inside the clasp!

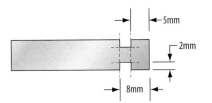

5mm
2mm
8mm

fig. 2

U

For this 25mm box, the tongue strip should be about 8x35mm long. Trim the strip to size. Use dividers to scribe lines to define the tab **[fig. 2]** and cut the small notches with shears **[U]**. File the corners inside the notches with barrette and square files. Cut the corners of the tab at 45 degrees **[V]**. Blend the corners into a half-round shape with the barrette file. Texture the tab to match the box clasp **[W]**.

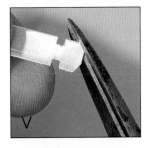

V

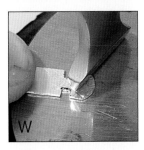

W

Solder a 6mm 18-gauge sterling jump ring closed with medium sterling solder. Flux the tongue and place it textured side down on the charcoal block. Add the jump ring, with the join over the end of the tab. Use easy solder. Heat the tongue first, bringing the heat down to the jump ring. Don't dwell on the join until the very end when the silver glows a light pink and the solder starts to melt. Quench, pickle, and rinse.

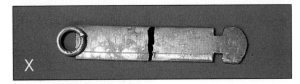

X

Dry the tongue and draw a marker line down the midpoint of the back (the side with the jump ring) **[X]**. Hold with flat or chainnose pliers, with the edge of the jaw along the black line. Fold the clasp in half—so it's not quite folded flat but about three-quarters of the way. Hammer the crease with a polished, slightly curved hammer face **[Y]**. This will flatten the crease and work-harden the silver to give it some spring. Bend the neck and tab 90 degrees away from the jump ring. Bend the tab back so it's parallel to the jump ring **[Z]**.

Y

Z

STEP 7: ADJUST THE FIT OF THE TONGUE

Often the clasp needs adjustment before it will work properly. Make sure the sides of the keyhole are straight and even and the corners are crisp, filing if necessary **[AA]**. Compare the width of the tongue with the keyhole. If it's too tight, file whichever is easier to match, the tongue or the keyhole. Check the narrow part of the keyhole against the neck of the tongue. File either one if the neck is too wide to pop up easily. Try adjusting the angle of the neck with pliers. Sometimes if it's too steep, it won't pop up.

Similarly, if the top of the keyhole is too shallow, the tongue won't have room to snap in place. Raise it up with a needle file. If the tongue is too long, cut it at the fold, shorten it, and solder it back together flat on a charcoal block. Fold the tongue and hammer

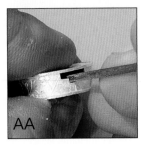

AA

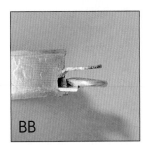

BB

again after pickling. If it's too flat, the tongue will slip out. Try opening the angle of the fold with pliers and increasing the spring-tension with a little more hammering. When it fits correctly, the tongue should snap in and the shoulders should pop up behind the narrow part of the hole, locking the clasp **[BB]**. To release the catch, push down on the tab.

STEP 8: FINISHING

Dry completely before finishing. Polish the clasp mostly with radial disks, starting with 120- or 220-grit to strip off any firescale and aligning the bristles of the wheels with the texture.

Koi Fish Pin

This pin takes sweat-soldering to the next level. With this much soldering, firescale could be rampant. But by using a firescale-preventative flux, the copper and sterling are still in brilliant shape at the end of the project and polishing couldn't be easier! Paint the scales with iridescent color with a brush of your flame.

techniques

Sweat-soldering
Soldering on a pin back
Using firescale preventative flux
Adding color to metal with a torch

tools

All tool sets plus nail set
with cupped end
Jumbo butane torch

materials

1½x2 in. (38x51mm) 24-gauge sterling sheet
2x2 in. (51x51mm) 24-gauge copper sheet
Easy sterling solder
Firescoff flux
1¾ in. (44mm) nickel pin stem, catch, and join
Rubber cement
Finishing coat (optional)

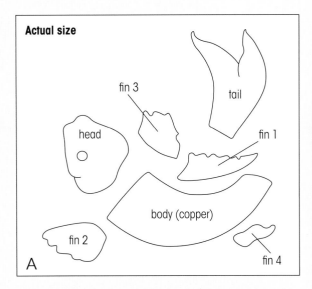

Actual size

fin 3

tail

head

fin 1

body (copper)

fin 2

fin 4

A

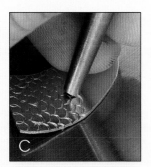

B

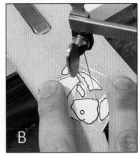

C

D

E

F

STEP 1: SAW OR SHEAR, STAMP, AND TEXTURE

Copy and glue the pattern **[A]** to the respective metals. Use French shears or a jeweler's saw to cut out the pieces. If you have experience sawing, a 2/0 or 4/0 blade can easily follow the lines of the design as you saw the pieces free **[B]**, with minimal filing to remove any excess metal, and you will be able to cut in the small detail line to suggest the gills. Otherwise, cut around the outlines with shears and file to the black outlines afterward.

After filing the pieces to match the patterns, remove the paper. Use a cross-peen hammer to texture the sterling tail and fin. For the body of the fish, practice making rows of scales on scrap metal until you're happy with the design before stamping your final piece. For the scales, use a cupped nail set as used in the Mixed-Metals Pendant. Tilt the stamp slightly away from the pattern to make half-round scales **[C]**. With each new row, shift the stamp so the mark is centered between two scales in the previous row. Leave the sterling head without texture.

STEP 2: SOLDER ON THE TAIL

Firescoff has to be applied to warm metal. Working on the solder board, place a drop of flux on the texture side of the tail **[D]**. Warm the metal lightly with the jumbo torch until the water boils away, leaving a white powder **[E]**. Continue adding flux and warming the metal until one side is covered **[F]**. Flip the piece over with tweezers. If it gets stuck to the board, warm it gently until it loosens. Repeat to cover the back. Don't let the metal get too hot before it's coated in flux, or firescale will start to form. Repeat to cover both sides of the copper body, ending on the back.

tip

Stop firescale before it happens by using Firescoff, a ceramic anti-firescale flux. No other flux is necessary. Firescoff rinses off in warm water, which means you can use it without pickle. By reducing firescale, it drastically reduces the labor it takes to polish the metal. Although it's more expensive than normal flux, you'll save on pickle and use fewer polishing abrasives. The manufacturers sell it in a spray bottle, but spraying it is messy and wasteful; this flux becomes sticky on surfaces, and that's not a good option when you're working at your kitchen table. Instead, transfer Firescoff to a bottle with a needle dispenser.

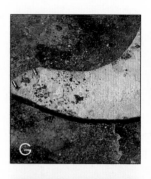

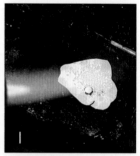

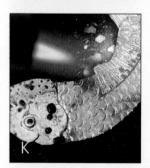

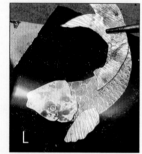

Place three double-length chips of easy solder on the back of the copper piece, where it will overlap the tail **[G]**. Melt the solder flat to the copper. Place the silver tail on the charcoal block. Flip the copper piece over with your tweezers and set it on top of the silver tail, solder side down. Heat both pieces evenly to sweat-solder the pieces together. Stand by with the pick in case anything shifts or if you have to press them together lightly during soldering **[H]**.

STEP 3: SOLDER ON THE EYE AND HEAD

Set the body and tail aside for a minute while you cut a large dot from leftover 24-gauge sterling sheet with the metal punch. Coat the eye and head with Firescoff as described in step 2. Melt a small chip of easy solder on the back of the dot. Sweat-solder the eye to the front of the head **[I]**. Flip the head over and melt 4–5 double lengths of solder along the edge that will lay on the copper.

Flip the head over with tweezers and place it on the body. Heat the pieces evenly until they are sweat-soldered **[J]**. If any charcoal sticks to the flux and could get in the way, either remove it with the tweezers or pick and touch up any missing spots with more Firescoff, or stop, quench, and pickle the piece. Flux it again and continue where you left off. In any case, when you're done soldering the head and tail, quench, pickle for a few minutes, and rinse. Firescoff can be removed with warm water, but why not use the extra cleaning power of the pickle to scrub your pieces?

STEP 4: SOLDER THE FINS TO THE BODY

Use the same techniques from steps 2 and 3 to sweat-solder the four fin pieces to the body. Coat both sides of all the parts and the body of the fish with flux. First you'll solder on the fins that attach to the front of the koi fish. (The other two fins attach to the back of the koi. Keep the textured side in mind as you solder; it's easy to solder on the wrong side!) Place 4–5 chips of easy solder on the back of fin 1 and melt them flat. Sweat-solder the fin to the copper body **[K]**. Melt two chips of solder along the top edge of the back of the large fin that sits near the head (fin 2). Raise the body with the third hand so that the pieces lay flat together, if necessary, and solder them **[L]**. Quench, pickle, and rinse.

Use a marker or scribe to outline the areas where the fins attach to the back of the copper **[M]**. Flux the fish again. The remaining fin pieces should still be fluxed from earlier but, if not, flux them again. Melt two chips inside each of the areas outlined on the copper. Attach fin 3 near the head **[N]**. Then angle the body with the third hand and solder fin 4 near the tail **[O]**. Quench, pickle, and rinse.

STEP 5: BEND THE FISH TO ADD DIMENSION
Use your fingers to gently round the dead-soft copper body of the fish toward the back **[P]**. Bend the fins and tail, too, with your fingers or nylon-jaw pliers. **[Q]**

STEP 6: SOLDER THE PIN FINDINGS TO THE BACK
The pin crosses the open space between the tail and the head, but will be hidden when worn. Separate parts for a pin include the stem, catch, and joint **[R]**. Nickel parts will create a long-lasting and durable pin.

Lay the pin stem on the back of the fish and outline with a marker where the joint and catch will go **[S]**. The joint will hold the round, riveted end of the stem. The catch should be a little below the tip of the stem. Lightly burnish the outlines on the copper with a scribe or permanent marker, and draw a short line in each circle to indicate the direction of the stem to help you line up the parts while soldering.

Flux the fish and place it upside down on the charcoal block. Don't flux the catch or joint; if solder floods the small parts, the mechanism may not work. When the bottom is in contact with the fluxed fish, it will have enough protection to flow. By not fluxing the rest of the findings, solder will be less likely to flow onto them even if they get a little too hot.

Support any fins that are raised above the block with a third hand so they don't fall during soldering. Place a small chip of easy solder inside the outline for the pin joint and melt it flat. Place the pin joint, using the scribed line as a guide to align it. Keep in it in place as you sweat-solder. Heat mostly the fish, bringing the red glow to the copper before the nickel glows red. Repeat for the pin catch **[T]**.

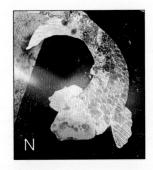
N

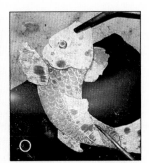
O

P

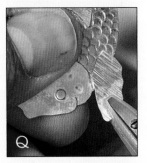
Q

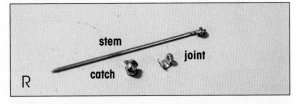
R
stem
joint
catch

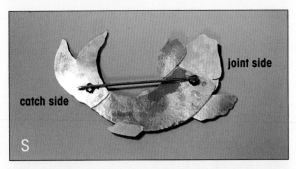
S
joint side
catch side

T

STEP 7: POLISH THE KOI FISH

Before attaching the pin stem, polish and patina the fish. Even before polishing, the sterling and copper look pretty good—almost completely free of firescale! **[U]** Use white or black silicone polishing wheels to remove any excess solder on the flat surfaces. Polish any discoloration and scratches away and clean up the texture with radial disks **[V]**. Soften the edges of the fins to create rounded bevels. First, bevel along their edges with the black silicone wheel **[W]**. Then polish them with the blue silicone wheel. Blend the finish by repeating the last round of radial disks. The bevels outline the texture and bounce the light in different directions **[X]**.

STEP 8: ADD PATINA WITH THE TORCH

Metal changes color as it's heated. The surface will change from straw gold to orange, then red to cobalt blue, before turning black. The color changes very quickly and continues after you remove the heat.

Clean the koi thoroughly of any polishing residue. Don't use any flux. Hold the fish with cross-locking tweezers **[Y]** and heat the copper lightly with the transparent brush of the flame. As soon as any color starts to appear, remove the flame and wait. Watch the colors continue to form. Repeat until satisfied with the patina. Let it air cool. Pickle the fish if you want to remove the color and try again.

Repeat the last step of polishing with the radial disks to remove any patina on the sterling parts for more contrast. Be careful not to brush the copper or the patina will be removed.

If you like, you can seal the patina with a coat of jewelry shield, Renaissance wax, or light coats of spray-on satin gloss polyurethane, but be aware that colors may not remain as vibrant, especially on copper.

STEP 9: ATTACH THE PIN STEM

Place the ball of the stem between the leaves of the pin joint and gently close them with chainnose pliers **[Z]**. The rivet should slip into the holes as you close the joint. Check the fit with the catch.

Bezel-Set Stone Ring

A bezel setting is a collar of metal that wraps around the stone and traps it, usually against a base. Bezels are one of the oldest stone settings and, in a way, they form the foundation of all other settings (including prongs, tube setting, flush setting, and so on). A bezel setting can be used in earrings, pendants, and clasps as well.

techniques
Making a bezel setting
Soldering a setting onto a backing
Setting a stone

tools
All tool sets plus tapered
    steel ring mandrel,
    curved steel burnisher
Jumbo butane torch

materials
2x2 in. (51x51mm) 20-gauge sterling sheet
12 in. (30.5cm) plain 28- or 30-gauge fine silver bezel strip
    (⅛, ³⁄₁₆, or ¼ in./3, 5, or 6.5mm wide)
12 in. 10-gauge half-round sterling wire
Easy sterling solder
Medium sterling solder
Cabochon
Dental floss
Scrap leather

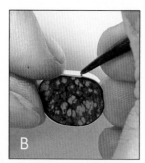

STEP 1: FORM THE BEZEL AROUND THE STONE

Your stone is the template for a custom-made setting. For your first bezel project, I recommend a round, oval, or slightly irregular shape stone. (Even round or oval stones are often slightly irregular, so you'll have to check the shape of the bezel against the stone often.) Avoid stones that have sharp corners. For more help with choosing a stone to set and matching it to bezel wire, see "How to Choose a Stone and Bezel Wire" on p. 99.

Fine silver bezel wire is very soft. Don't crush it while you wrap it around the stone. Keep the girdle of the stone in the middle of the bezel strip. Work with the flat back of the stone facing you as much as possible, because that is the widest part and the clearest view of the shape for most stones.

Use your flush-cutters or French shears to trim the end of the bezel wire to a straight, right angle. Start with the trimmed end of the wire in the middle of one side of the stone **[A]**. On ovals or irregular stones, I prefer the longest side. On a round stone, it doesn't matter where you start.

Hold the end of the wire in place with one finger. Wrap the rest of the bezel around the stone, either in your hand or with the stone resting on the table. Hold the long tail of the bezel wire

in your hand with some tension, so the bezel stays snug. Look for any gaps and adjust the fit. Keep the bezel sides straight while you shift your grip to one hand and mark with a scribe or felt pen where to cut the bezel **[B]**.

Use your shears or flush-cutters to trim the bezel to size, cutting at a right angle. Place the bezel on the stone and check the fit. The ends should meet or have only a slight gap. If they still overlap, trim again. It's better if the bezel is the right size or slightly too small, since it's easy to stretch it later. If it's too big, you'll have to cut the bezel open, size it, and solder again. File the join carefully with a flat needle file, if necessary, or nibble a little off with flush-cutters. Hold the thin wire steady in your fingers as you work to avoid rounding the corners. Check the fit again after any filing or trimming.

Use half-round pliers to adjust the angle of each side of the join for a better fit. Make sure the edges meet evenly. Overlap the ends over and under each other to close the join with tension. If you can't get the bezel to stay together on its own, use two third hands to hold the join together. On either side of the join, grip it with just the tips of the cross-locking tweezers as far from the seam as possible.

STEP 2: SOLDER THE BEZEL WIRE CLOSED

Since fine silver doesn't get firescale, flux just both sides of the join with paste flux. Hold the bezel on the side opposite the seam with tweezers. Be careful not to open the join as you place it on a charcoal block with the seam facing you. Cut a few small chips of medium sterling solder. Ball the solder up and scoop it up on the tip of a clean pick. Warm the bezel, heating the side away from the join and then the seam repeatedly, until the flux clears. As it clears, keep the bezel warm while you touch the solder ball to the top of the join until it sticks **[C]**. It has to sit on the line or it will flood one side of the bezel and not work! Heat the back of the bezel again and then bring the heat to the front, focusing the flame on the center of the seam. Repeat, dwelling longer and longer on the seam, until the solder flows.

After soldering, quench, pickle, and rinse the bezel. You should see a clear line of solder from top to bottom on both sides. Resolder if necessary. File away any excess solder on the inside of the bezel with a needle file. Don't remove any extra solder from the outside yet; it will help to protect the join from opening during later soldering.

STEP 3: RESHAPE THE BEZEL

The bezel is often distorted after soldering. Gently shaping an oval or irregular bezel on a round mandrel can remove any waves or bumps in the metal, making it look nicer. And, when you shape it around the stone, you can move the join line to a better place. For example, if you make a pendant, you can hide the join by placing it where the jump ring or bail will be attached.

To move the join or straighten the bezel, place it on a ring mandrel and tap it around the circumference gently with a rawhide mallet. Remove it, reverse the bezel, and repeat one more time. Be careful not to stretch it any larger. If the bezel is fine, skip this step and use just the stone to reshape it.

If your bezel is not round, open it from the inside with chainnose or half-round pliers **[D]**. Look at the back side of the stone with the bezel on it **[E]**. Check for gaps. If the bezel is too loose, cut it open at the join and resize it.

Rest the bezel on your table and insert the stone. Pull the bezel off, and repeat. The stone should slip in without a lot of pressure, and the bezel should come off easily. Pressing too hard will flare the bottom and distort the bezel, and it might not fit after soldering it to the base.

If the stone is a little snug in the setting, repeatedly putting the stone in and taking it out will stretch the soft fine silver to size. If the stone won't fit at all or is crooked, put the bezel back on a mandrel and *planish* it by tapping lightly around the join with a polished steel hammer with a slightly rounded face. Tap in a row on both sides of the join and check the fit. If it doesn't fit, reverse the bezel on the mandrel, and repeat another set of rows just outside the first set. Don't hammer in the same spot or you can thin the bezel too much. Check the bezel on the stone; repeat until the bezel fits.

STEP 4: SAND THE EDGES OF THE BEZEL FLAT

In order to solder the bezel onto a piece of sheet metal, the bottom of the bezel must be flat. Gently sand the top and bottom edges on 320-grit sandpaper.

Turn the bezel often as you work so that you don't taper it. Place the stone in your bezel again to correct it, in case it was distorted during sanding. If your stone only fits the bezel in

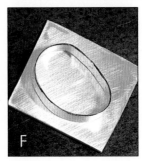

one direction, clearly mark the top edge with a felt pen. Place the bezel bottom down on a truly flat surface, such as your steel bench block. When you're done, there should be no gaps between the edge and the steel—only just a little light.

STEP 5: CUT SHEET METAL FOR THE BEZEL BOTTOM

Use a piece of 20-gauge sterling sheet for the bottom of the setting. In silver, 20-gauge is the thickest that will cut easily with shears, and it's great for a deep, stamped border. If you want a thicker edge for your setting, you can use 18- or 16-gauge, but you will need to cut it with a jeweler's saw. For a flush bezel with no border, use thinner sheet metal, such as 24-gauge.

Use dividers to measure a square around your bezel that is at least ⅛ in. (3.2mm) larger on all sides. The base must be larger for easy soldering and to form the decorative edge later. Cut the base out with French shears. Flatten it on the steel block with a rawhide mallet. Check your sheet against the steel block. If it's still not flat, gently tap the raised areas down with the nearly flat face of a polished steel hammer. Check the fit between the bezel and sheet metal on your steel block. If there are still gaps, and the bezel alone is flat on the steel block, then the sheet metal is the problem. Either sand one side of the sheet metal flat on 320-grit paper, or anneal the metal, pickle it, and flatten it again when it's dead soft. Check the fit again and repeat until the seam is free of gaps **[F]**.

G

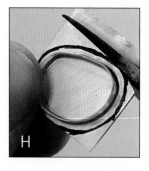

H

I

STEP 6: SOLDER THE BEZEL TO THE BASE

Check the fit of the stone again. You don't want to solder it in place only to realize afterwards that the bezel doesn't fit the stone any more! Using a soldering tripod, set up the bezel so that you can heat the sheet metal from underneath. Or hold one edge of the sheet with a third hand. Move the setup close to the edge of the table so you can angle the torch upward easily. This will avoid melting your bezel and will help draw the solder down and around the seam. Keep your work over the tile and solder board for safety, not hanging over the edge of the table and your lap!

Use a jumbo torch for all but the smallest bezels (less than ½ in./1.3cm in diameter). The large flame will help heat thick sheet metal bases and the steel mesh of the tripod. If you use a third hand, hold the sheet metal along the edge with the least amount of tweezer. Level the setting so it doesn't slide during soldering. And don't let the tweezers touch the seam or solder, or you might solder them to the bezel! Raise the third-hand base on a charcoal block or another flameproof surface to allow more room for the torch.

Cut 8–10 double-length pieces of easy solder wire. Apply flux or Firescoff with heat to completely coat both sides of the base. For the fine silver bezel, apply flux just to the join again. The bottom edge will pick up flux from the sheet metal. Heat underneath the sheet metal with a low flame to clear the flux

and let the bezel settle into place. Push it into position with the pick, making sure there is enough room for a border on all sides. Keep the metal warm from underneath as you place solder evenly around the outside of the bezel [G]. Move the flame aside to a safe neutral position each time you place a chip of solder. Warm the flux again to stick the solder in place after each chip. Start with one piece at the bezel join. Each piece of solder should be about ¼ in. (6.4mm) from the previous piece. Make sure the solder is touching the seam and resting on the sheet metal. Placing solder on the inside of the bezel can cause trouble later; lumps that are left behind may prevent the stone from fitting well.

Turn the torch up to increase the heat and bring it back under the setting. Move it slowly and evenly, staying inside the edges of the sheet metal, with the tip of the cone very close to the metal. Watch for the solder to flow completely around and then stop. Quench, pickle for 5–10 minutes, and rinse.

STEP 7: TRIM AND FILE THE BASE TO SIZE

From this point on, don't insert the stone into the setting without dental floss underneath or it will get stuck! Using floss is a handy trick to help you remove the stone if it sticks in the bezel: Simply pull up on both sides of the floss to remove the stone.

Dry the setting. Drape a piece or two of dental floss over the setting, then check the fit of the stone inside the bezel again. Draw a border around the bezel with a marker, leaving about a ⅛ in. (3.2mm) border to allow room for stamping a design. You could also set dividers to the width of the border and, resting one leg against the outside of the bezel, scribe an outline around the setting. Trim with shears [H] or use a jeweler's saw. File the shape and then the edges to smooth them [I].

STEP 8: STAMP A DESIGN

Practice stamping on a piece of scrap metal before working on your border. Using design stamps, create a decorative pattern around the border of your setting. Combine two or more stamps (such as lines and circles) to make more interesting patterns. Take care to avoid crushing or marring the bezel! Stamping can distort the edge. File around the edge again to remove any sharp points. Set the bezel setting aside while you make the shank for the ring.

STEP 9: MAKE THE RING SHANK

You will use many of the techniques you learned in the textured ring project. Use 10-gauge sterling half-round wire to make two rings and solder them together to make a wider band. Refer to the Ring Blank Size by Metal Gauge table on p. 108 to find the length of your ring blank. Cross-reference your size with the gauge of the metal; note that 10-gauge half-round wire is approximately 1.3mm thick, or the equivalent of 16-gauge.

Form the ring with a mallet and mandrel **[J]**. Close the join with half-round pliers **[K]**. File with a flat file for a better seam, if necessary. Solder the ring closed using the jumbo torch, Firescoff, and medium sterling solder wire. It may take two small balls of solder to fill the join. Repeat to make a second ring to match. Quench, pickle, and rinse.

Sand one side of each ring flat on 320-grit sandpaper on a flat surface. Flux both rings with Firescoff. Place one ring, flat side up, on the charcoal block, warm the ring to clear the flux, and place eight balls of medium solder evenly around the edge **[L]**. Melt the solder flat to the edge of the ring. Stack the second ring on top with the flat sides together and the joins of both rings aligned **[M]**. Continue heating until the rings settle against each other and solder flows around the seam. Quench, pickle, and rinse.

STEP 10: SWEAT-SOLDER THE RING TO THE SETTING

Use the flat side of a large medium-cut file to make a flat spot at the top of the ring where the joins are aligned **[N]**. Test the fit between the ring and the back of the setting before you add flux **[O]**. Use a scribe to make guidelines on the back of the setting to help you place the solder and the ring during soldering.

Cut 3–4 double-length chips of easy solder and flux them. Flux the setting and ring with Firescoff. Place the setting upside down on the charcoal block, clear the flux, and melt two chips of easy solder on the back, inside the guidelines where the flat part of the ring will sit **[P]**. Hold the ring by the bottom of the shank with a third hand, then place the flat spot down on the back of the setting on top of the solder. Check it against your guidelines and make sure it is centered in all directions **[Q]**. There should be just enough downward pressure to help the ring fall into place when the solder flows. Continue heating

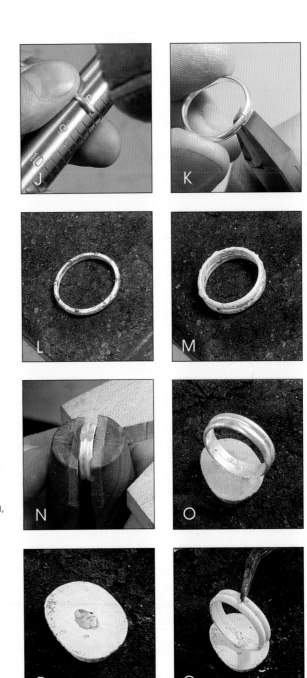

R

S

until the solder flows and the ring sweat-solders to the setting. Quench, pickle for 20 minutes or more to remove as much firescale as possible, and rinse.

Check the join. Make sure that the ring is soldered completely flat against the back of the setting. Since this is the last soldered join before setting the stone, check the rest of the joins for any problems that may have occurred during fabrication and should be fixed before continuing.

STEP 11: POLISH AND ADD PATINA

Before you set your stone, you should polish the ring [R]. and add patina, if desired [S].

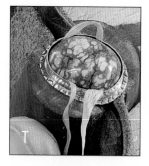

T

U

Polish only inside the setting if your stone is clear or semi-transparent and would be set off by a bright, mirror shine. With stones that are clear or semi-clear, be careful with patina. Apply it just to the areas you want to antique, such as the border and the recess between the banded rings; don't let it get under the stone or it can dull the shine and change the appearance of the stone. Of course, that's not a problem with a solid, opaque stone!

V

W

Remove the patina from the highlights with another round of extra-fine polishing or a polishing pad. Make sure the ring is clean of all polishing residue and any patina is neutralized before setting the stone.

STEP 12: SET THE STONE

The moment of truth has arrived: It's stone-setting time! Use a scrap of clean leather around the shank to keep the ring from being marred when holding it in the ring clamp. Brace the ring clamp in the V-slot of your bench pin for support.

X

When setting a stone in a bezel, you will push down or burnish only the top third of the bezel, not the entire side of it. Don't push the bezel in one continuous line around the stone; doing that can create a wrinkle of metal that is very difficult to burnish down. Instead, work your way around the stone, crimping one spot, then moving to the spot directly opposite.

Y

First, place floss across the setting and insert the stone to check the fit one last time [T]. The stone should fit all the way down to the bottom. If the bezel has been pushed in, use the burnisher to carefully push it back out from the inside of the setting. If the stone is very low, you can raise it with some padding—sawdust, a plastic lid, cardboard, or paper will work (as long as the stone is opaque).

Remove the floss and reinsert the stone. Hold the burnisher over your finger and against the top third of the bezel, with the tip curved away from the stone. Try to pivot on your fingertip and push with control so you don't slip and scratch the stone. Press down on one spot, which we'll call north **[U]**. Next, crimp the opposite side, or south. Then crimp in between at east and then west **[V]**. Continue to push down wherever the metal

is sticking up, in pairs of opposites, until the entire bezel is flush against the stone **[W]**. Turn the burnisher and rub it hard against the top edge (avoiding the stone) to burnish away small lumps, smoothing and polishing the bezel **[X]**.

Take care so you don't scratch your ring with the burnisher's sharp tip. Work one quarter of the bezel, then work the opposite side. Repeat until the bezel is smooth, there are no gaps, and the stone is tight in the setting **[Y]**. Carefully polish away any remaining bumps or scratches, positioning your hands so that you don't slip and scratch the stone. Clean the ring.

How to Choose a Stone and Bezel Wire

CHOOSE A TOUGH STONE

For your first bezel settings, avoid soft stones. Every stone has a rating from 1–10 on the Mohs scale; 1 is the softest and easiest to scratch, and 10 is the hardest. Garnets, amethyst, quartz, agate, and jasper are durable, scratch-resistant, and good for beginners. As you work with more stones and gain experience, you'll learn about other qualities such as cracking and flaking.

MOHS HARDNESS SCALE	
1	Talc
2	Pearl, Amber, Cinnabar
3	Coral
4	Jet
5	Turquoise, Opal, Apatite, Lapis
6	Garnet, Sugilite
7	Jasper, Amethyst, Quartz
8	Spinel, Topaz, Zirconia
9	Ruby, Sapphire
10	Diamond

Cabochons are the easiest to set with bezels. A well-cut cab tapers from the edge as it rises to the top of the stone. The bottom should be flat with little or no rounding. Bullets are tall cabs—so tall that they can pull out of your setting and are difficult to bezel without using a little glue. Some cabs are cut very thin, with narrow edges, and require extra work to set. What you're looking for in a well-cut cab is a nice profile to the stone that makes for an easy bezel setting. Place a straight edge against the stone's profile and look for the kind of angle illustrated by the arrow.

MATCH BEZEL WIRE TO STONE

The easiest bezel wire to use is made from 28- or 30-gauge fine silver. It's available with straight,

scalloped, and serrated edges. Bezel wire is sold in different heights including ⅛ in. (3.2mm), ³⁄₁₆ in. (4.8mm), and ¼ in. (6.4mm). You'll also find stepped bezel wire, which makes its own base, and some with built-in borders and intricate pierced patterns that are usually made of sterling, which is harder to set.

Hold the bezel wire against the edge of the stone and close one eye as you measure it. The height of the bezel wire should be a little above where the edge of the stone starts to taper toward the top.

If the stone is too short for the only bezel wire you have on hand, you can carefully trim the wire to size or raise your stone with a little padding—some thin plastic or cardboard will work.

Butterfly Pendant

This project combines many of the soldering skills learned so far to make a pendant with a floral arrangement of leaves, stems, and a butterfly. You can easily change the small components that are assembled inside the frame to make your own designs.

techniques
Soldering seams
Sweat soldering
Tapering wire

tools
All tool sets plus tapered steel ring mandrel
Micro and jumbo torches

materials
6 in. (15.2cm) 16-gauge sterling round wire
6 in. 18-gauge sterling round wire
6 in. 16-gauge copper round wire
1½x1½ in. (38x38mm) 24-gauge sterling sheet
1x1 in. (25.5x25.5mm) 26-gauge patterned sterling sheet
2 6mm OD 18-gauge sterling jump rings
Easy sterling solder
Medium sterling solder

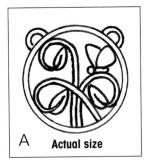

A

Actual size

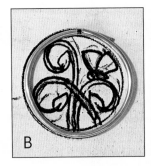

B

C

D

E

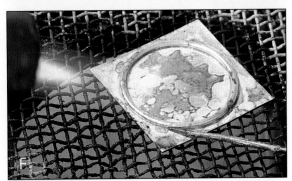

F

STEP 1: CREATE A FRAME FOR THE PENDANT

Use the pattern **[A]** as a guide for making all the parts for this pendant, which is 1 in. (25.5mm) in diameter. Using the formula you learned in the box clasp project, calculate the length of 16-gauge wire needed to make the frame. In this project, it would be 3.14 x 1 in. (25.5mm) = 3.14 in. (80mm). The thicker the wire, the longer it will have to be to match after closing the join and soldering, so round the length up to 3¼ in. (83mm).

Trim the wire ends flush before measuring and cut the wire to size. Form the wire around a ring mandrel. The ends should overlap. Place the wire on your sketch and squeeze the ends together until the size matches the sketch. Mark the trim **[B]** and cut the wire again, making both sides of the join flush.

Close the ring and flux it for soldering. I recommend using Firescoff for this entire project, which will minimize firescale for less polishing later. Flux the ring completely. Solder with a small ball of medium solder. Warm the ring away from the join and then swing the heat up to the join. Repeat until the silver starts to glow a light pink, then focus the flame on the join until the solder flows. Quench, pickle, and rinse. Dry the ring, reshape it on the mandrel with a mallet, then flatten it on a steel block with the mallet. Reverse it and flatten it again.

STEP 2: CUT THE BLANK FOR THE BACKGROUND

Use dividers to take a measurement a little wider than the diameter of the wire pendant frame. Scribe a matching square on a piece of 24-gauge sterling sheet and cut it out with shears. Flatten it with the steel block and mallet. Sand the bottom of the wire frame flat on 320-grit sandpaper. Check the fit between the frame and the backing on a flat steel block **[C]**. If there are any gaps, check the frame against the true flat surface of the steel block. If it looks fine, you may have to sand the sheet metal on one side to make it fit.

STEP 3: SOLDER THE BACKING TO THE FRAME

Flux all sides of the frame and backing. Place them on the tripod, with the frame centered on the sheet metal. Heating from below with the large torch, warm the flux until it turns clear and keep it warm while you place 8–10 double-length chips of medium solder around the outside of the seam. Be sure to place one near the join of the ring. Continue heating from below until the sterling glows a light red and the solder starts to glow **[D]**. Move the torch to heat the silver from above, watching for the solder to flow in a complete circle around the frame **[E]**. If there are small gaps, drag the molten solder across them with the tip of the pick **[F]**. Quench and pickle.

Check for gaps, tap them closed with a mallet on the steel block, and solder again, placing a new chip of solder near each gap. Quench, pickle, rinse, and dry. Using shears, trim the

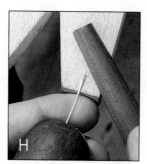

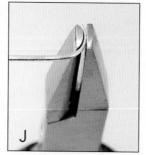

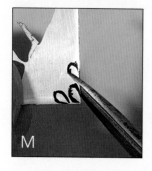

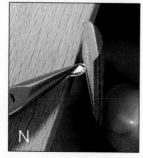

with a ring clamp to keep the wire from turning as you file. With your finger, support the end on the bench pin **[H]**. It's easier to file a taper by making the wire square first. File four flat sides on the wire, creating a square profile, on just the ¹/₂ in. you're tapering. Then file more toward the tip, working evenly on each side, and taper it to a blunt point **[I]**. To round the wire again, turn the wire to rest on the corners and file the corners flat on all sides, making the wire octagonal. Blend the corners away with light filing to make the wire round again.

Referring to the pattern, bend the tapered end of the wire with half-round pliers to curl an end **[J]**. Place the wire on the pattern and use the pliers and your fingers to adjust the wire to match the drawing **[K]**. Cut the wire a little longer than the sketch so that it can be trimmed to size later. Repeat to create the other two stems.

Place the two background stems in position on the backing, with the curves touching the borders and the ends over the point where the ring is joined. Mark the trim point with a marker **[L]** and trim the ends flush.

STEP 5: CUT AND SOLDER THE LEAVES
Each wire stem ends with a leaf in the form of a simple teardrop shape cut from 24-gauge sterling sheet. Following the pattern, sketch the leaves on the sheet metal with a felt pen. It's OK if they are all a bit different in size and shape—in fact, it will look more natural. Rough-cut the leaf shapes with shears **[M]**. File to refine the shapes, holding the leaf with chainnose pliers and bracing against your bench pin **[N]**. Match the leaves with the stems and check them against the pattern.

Flux one of the sets and place the leaf stem on the solder board. Warm the pieces with the micro torch until the flux clears and use the tweezers or pick to adjust their position, if necessary. Place a small ball of medium solder against the stem and leaf **[O]**. Heat the two pieces evenly until the solder flows down the seam, joining them. Repeat for the other two sets. Refer to the pattern as you work so that you solder the stems and leaves with the right orientation! Quench, pickle, rinse, and dry.

STEP 6: SOLDER THE STEMS TO THE FRAME
Flatten the stems and leaves with the mallet and steel block. Flux the pendant and the two stems that will rest on the

excess metal close to the wire **[G]**, but wait to file until later to keep any extra solder in place, so the seam won't get pits during later soldering.

STEP 4: SHAPE WIRES FOR THE STEMS
To create the design for the floral stems, taper the ends of the 18-gauge wire pieces and use half-round pliers to match the shapes in the pattern. Flush-cut the end of a piece of 18-gauge wire and file a tapered point on the last ½ in. (13mm). Hold it

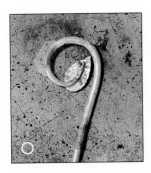

backing. Place them on the charcoal block or tripod and warm them with the large torch until the flux clears. Place small balls of easy solder where the stems touch the frame **[P]**. Bring the flame closer to the pendant and move in a slow spiral over the metal until the solder starts to flow. Focus on each join in turn as the balls flow, soldering the stems to the border. Place a small ball of easy solder next to each leaf. Make sure the leaves are flat on the metal. Repeat the slow spiral to tack the leaves in place. Quench, pickle for a few minutes, and rinse.

Place the third stem on the pendant, curving it so it drapes over the other two stems and touches the sides of the border. The leaf should be flat against the sheet metal, and the stem should rest on the stems of the pair beneath it. Where it touches the border, mark the stem with a felt pen **[Q]** and trim it flush. Repeat the steps above to solder the third stem to the frame. Place three small balls of easy solder: one on each end of the stem where it touches the border, and one to solder the stem to the pair below in the middle **[R]**. After the stem is soldered, put another small ball of easy solder next to the leaf to tack it down to the backing.

Work on the tripod or off the edge of the charcoal block to bring heat under the pendant, which will speed up soldering and help draw the solder into the join. Heat the block and silver underneath the edge **[S]**. Bring the heat over the pendant to heat it from the top, too. Alternate between the top and bottom until the stem and leaf are soldered in place. Use tweezers to turn the pendant on the block if you need to focus heat under another part. Quench, pickle, and rinse the pendant.

STEP 7: MAKE A BUTTERFLY AND SOLDER TO THE PENDANT

Draw two wing shapes on some 26-gauge patterned sterling sheet metal with a permanent marker. (If you don't have patterned sterling, texture the metal first with hammers or

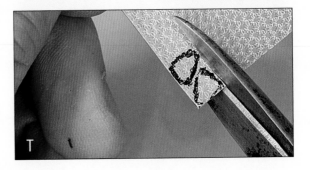

stamps.) Cut the wings out with shears **[T]**, file them to size, and set aside. To make the butterfly head and body, cut ⅛ in. (3.2mm) of 16-gauge copper wire and melt it into a ball. Use the jumbo torch because it takes a lot of heat to melt copper. Pickle for a few minutes and rinse. Flush-cut another ⅛-in. (3.2mm) piece of copper wire. Flux the ball and small piece of wire. Put them together on the solder board with the flat side of

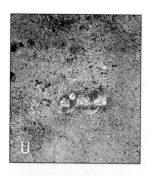

the ball facing down and place a tiny ball of medium solder on the join **[U]**. Solder the two together. Pickle and rinse.

Check the fit and arrangement of the butterfly in the pendant **[V]**. Note which wing should be on top and how they fit together. Adjust the size of the wings, if necessary. Flux the wings. Working on the solder board with the micro torch, melt a small chip of medium solder on the back of the top wing. Flip it over and place it solder side down on the bottom wing. Hold the wings in place with the pick while you solder **[W]**. Quench, pickle, and rinse.

Flux the pendant and the butterfly parts. Place the pendant on the tripod for sweat-soldering the butterfly in place. Heating the pendant from underneath will avoid melting or unsoldering the stems or butterfly. Warm the pendant until the flux clears, place two chips of easy solder where the butterfly will go **[X]**, and melt them flat. Place the body and wings on the pendant. Bring the tip of the flame's cone up under the mesh and move it in a slow circle under the pendant **[Y]**. As the red glow transfers from the steel to the silver, watch the butterfly for signs of soldering, such as sliver flowing out around the edges. When the piece glows light pink and it looks like the solder is flowing, bring the heat to the top of the pendant and heat for a few seconds more to make sure the butterfly is fully soldered. Quench, pickle, and rinse. If everything is still in place after pickling, you did it! If not, sweat-solder it again. Check all the joins carefully and fill any open seams with easy solder.

STEP 8: FILE THE EDGES AND ADD JUMP RINGS
To smooth the pendant edge, hold it in a ring clamp, brace it against the bench pin, and file across the edge to clean up the excess metal, solder, and the seam **[Z]**. File at a slight angle away from the border to preserve the shape of the round wire's profile. This will also create a bevel around the back.

Next you'll sweat-solder on two jump rings to keep the pendant from flipping around while worn. Close two 6mm jump rings with medium solder, and tack a second ball of easy solder to each one. Use the jumbo torch to focus the heat mostly on the pendant **[AA]** until the solder flows and the pendant falls, soldering the rings in place. Quench, pickle, and rinse. Check the strength of the jump ring joins and add more solder if necessary, working on the back of the pendant and propping the rings with a small piece of charcoal or a third hand. Polish and patinate the pendant.

Appendix

In this section, you'll find some extra information on ring sizing, a glossary of terms used throughout the book, and a few suggestions on reliable sources for jewelry-making tools and materials.

Sizing Rings

Use a finger gauge to determine ring size or measure the size of an existing ring on a steel mandrel.

MEASURING YOUR RING SIZE

Ring sizes in the U.S. range from 1–15 and higher. To find your ring size, either measure the size of an existing ring on a ring mandrel or size your finger with a finger gauge. A ring mandrel is a steel, wood, or plastic tapered cylinder that is made to match standard ring sizes and has corresponding measurements marked on it. For shaping and sizing precious-metal rings, use a steel mandrel.

On the mandrel, whole sizes are marked with a number with a line under it, such as <u>8</u>. The line between two whole sizes represents a half-size. Some mandrels will also have lines for quarter-sizes.

To measure a ring with a ring mandrel, place the ring on the mandrel as far as it will go. Measure the size at the center of the ring itself. For example, the band of a size 8 ring should be centered over the line for size 8.

A finger gauge is a set of rings calibrated to match standard sizes. Finger gauges can be plastic or metal, and thin or wide bands. A wide ring band will fit your finger differently than a thinner ring. A thin band can slip to the base of your finger, where it naturally tapers. A wide band fits over more of your finger and so has to be a little larger to fit comfortably. Whole sizes are marked with just the number and half sizes are marked with the number and a dash (8–).

When you use a finger gauge, the ring should turn easily on the finger and slip off with a little effort. If it's too tight to turn, it's the wrong size. If the gauge comes off too easily, it's too big. Fingers swell in the summer and shrink in the winter. A ring that's loose in summer will fall off in winter. A tight ring in winter may not come off at all in hot weather. If the gauge gets stuck on a finger, elevate the hand above the head and support the weight of the rest of the gauge. Use glass cleaner or olive oil to lubricate the finger gauge as you try to remove it. If your ring is the wrong size, you can stretch, planish, or add material to the ring to make it bigger. To shrink it, you can remove material.

INCREASING UP TO A HALF-SIZE WITH STRETCHING

Pull the ring down on the mandrel as far as it will go. Using the mallet, strike the ring with a downward stroke to force it to stretch a little. Hammer like this once around the entire ring. Remove and reverse the ring on the mandrel and repeat the hammering for one more round. Check the size and repeat as necessary. Stop when the ring lines up with the correct size on the mandrel.

INCREASING UP TO THREE-QUARTERS OF A SIZE WITH PLANISHING

Planishing by tapping the band with a steel hammer will thin it and stretch it faster and further than with a mallet. Place the ring on the mandrel as above and hammer lightly and evenly around the ring. Keep checking the size as you work, and reverse the ring after each round. For wider bands, you should concentrate your planishing on the edge of the ring that sits on the thick end of the mandrel. The other side sits above the tapering steel and if you hammer there you'll slant or "cone" your band, which will alter the fit and size, and tilt the ring.

INCREASING A SIZE OR MORE BY ADDING MATERIAL

If your ring is too thin, delicate or detailed to stretch by planishing, or if it has to be bigger than you can safely stretch, increase the size by adding material. Use the sizing chart on p. 108 to find the amount to add. Find the current size of your ring and the size you want on the chart. Set a pair of dividers to the distance between the two sizes. Use a matching shape and gauge of metal for your additional piece. Scribe the amount you need on the metal with the dividers and cut it with your pliers. Use a jeweler's saw to cut the ring open at the join, or, if the gauge is thin enough, cut with flush-cut pliers or shears. Make sure each side is flush. Insert the new material and pinch it in place with the edges of the join. Solder and reshape the ring as described in the textured ring project. File away any excess metal and the join to make any evidence of sizing disappear.

Stretch the ring with a rawhide mallet.

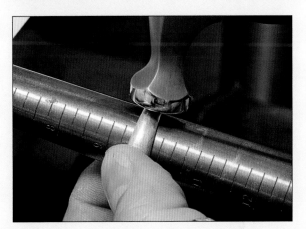

Planish with a steel hammer.

DECREASING BY REMOVING MATERIAL

To shrink your ring, you have to remove some of the band and solder the ring closed again. To find the right amount, use the sizing chart on p. 108. Find the current size of your ring and the size you want on the chart. Set a pair of dividers to the distance between the two sizes. Find the join on your ring and scribe the amount to remove with the dividers, either starting from the join or with the join in the middle of the amount to remove. Use a jeweler's saw or shears to remove the section of ring. You don't want to leave the original join elsewhere on the ring or it might fall apart while you're trying to solder the new one. Solder and reshape your ring as described in the textured ring project.

Sizing Rings

Use this table as a guide when you're cutting ring blank material from sheet metal. Match the size and gauge of the metal, then find the length you'll need to cut. Consider whether the ring will stretch and grow; if so, you may want to decrease the starting size. It's always a good idea to make a ring prototype first. The small chart below is a guide for determining how much material to add or remove when adjusting a ring size.

RING BLANK SIZE BY METAL GAUGE Thickness in millimeters (B&S gauge in parentheses)								
U.S. Size	**2.1 (12)**	**2.0**	**1.8**	**1.6 (14)**	**1.4**	**1.3 (16)**	**1.2**	**1 (18)**	**.8 (20)**
5	55.6	55.3	54.7	54.0	53.4	53.1	52.8	52.1	51.5
5.25	56.2	55.9	55.3	54.6	54.0	53.7	53.4	52.7	52.1
5.5	56.9	56.6	56.0	55.3	54.7	54.4	54.1	53.4	52.8
5.75	57.5	57.2	56.6	55.9	55.3	55.0	54.7	54.0	53.4
6	58.1	57.8	57.2	56.5	55.9	55.6	55.3	54.6	54.0
6.25	58.8	58.5	57.9	57.2	56.6	56.3	56.0	55.3	54.7
6.5	59.4	59.1	58.5	57.8	57.2	56.9	56.6	55.9	55.3
6.75	60.0	59.7	59.1	58.4	57.8	57.5	57.2	56.5	55.9
7	60.6	60.3	59.7	59.0	58.4	58.1	57.8	57.1	56.5
7.25	61.3	61.0	60.4	59.7	59.1	58.8	58.5	57.8	57.2
7.5	61.9	61.6	61.0	60.3	59.7	59.4	59.1	58.4	57.8
7.75	62.5	62.2	61.6	60.9	60.3	60.0	59.7	59.0	58.4
8	63.2	62.9	62.3	61.6	61.0	60.7	60.4	59.7	59.1
8.25	63.8	63.5	62.9	62.2	61.6	61.3	61.0	60.3	59.7
8.5	64.4	64.1	63.5	62.8	62.2	61.9	61.6	60.9	60.3
8.75	65.0	64.7	64.1	63.4	62.8	62.5	62.2	61.5	60.9
9	65.7	65.4	64.8	64.1	63.5	63.2	62.9	62.2	61.6
9.25	66.3	66.0	65.4	64.7	64.1	63.8	63.5	62.8	62.2
9.5	66.9	66.6	66.0	65.3	64.7	64.4	64.1	63.4	62.8
9.75	67.5	67.2	66.6	65.9	65.3	65.0	64.7	64.0	63.4
10	68.2	67.9	67.3	66.6	66.0	65.7	65.4	64.7	64.1
10.25	68.8	68.5	67.9	67.2	66.6	66.3	66.0	65.3	64.7
10.5	69.4	69.1	68.5	67.8	67.2	66.9	66.6	65.9	65.3
10.75	70.1	69.8	69.2	68.5	67.9	67.6	67.3	66.6	66.0
11	70.7	70.4	69.8	69.1	68.5	68.2	67.9	67.2	66.6
11.25	71.3	71.0	70.4	69.7	69.1	68.8	68.5	67.8	67.2
11.5	71.9	71.6	71.0	70.3	69.7	69.4	69.1	68.4	67.8
11.75	72.6	72.3	71.7	71.0	70.4	70.1	69.8	69.1	68.5
12	73.2	72.9	72.3	71.6	71.0	70.7	70.4	69.7	69.1
12.25	73.8	73.5	72.9	72.2	71.6	71.3	71.0	70.3	69.7
12.5	74.5	74.2	73.6	72.9	72.3	72.0	71.7	71.0	70.4
12.75	75.1	74.8	74.2	73.5	72.9	72.6	72.3	71.6	71.0
13	75.7	75.4	74.8	74.1	73.5	73.2	72.9	72.2	71.6
13.25	77.3	77.0	76.4	75.7	75.1	74.8	74.5	73.8	73.2
13.5	77.9	77.6	77.0	76.3	75.7	75.4	75.1	74.4	73.8
13.75	78.6	78.3	77.7	77.0	76.4	76.1	75.8	75.1	74.5
14	79.2	78.9	78.3	77.6	77.0	76.7	76.4	75.7	75.1

0 —

1 —
2 —
3 —
4 —
5 —
6 —
7 —
8 —
9 —
10 —
11 —
12 —
13 —
14 —
15 —
16 —

Glossary

Alloy A metal made by combining two or more pure metals. For example, sterling silver is an alloy of 92.5% silver and 7.5% copper. When cut, an alloy has no separate metals visible to the naked eye, unlike gold-filled, plated, or copper-core wires.

Annealing Metal is relaxed and returned to a dead soft, more malleable state by heating it, usually to a low red color. Different metals require different amounts of heat to anneal them, and vary as to whether or not they should be cooled quickly or slowly.

Argentium sterling silver An alloy of 92.5–93% fine silver and germanium. Since this sterling silver contains little to no copper, it can be fused easily, resists tarnish, and doesn't produce deep layers of fire stain when soldered. It has the same amount of silver or more as traditional sterling.

Bench pin A piece of hardwood that is clamped to your work table and is designed to support metal pieces as you work on them. Bench pins usually have a V-shaped cut in them to allow you to saw and maneuver the metal as you work.

Burnisher A tool used to polish silver and push bezel settings around gemstones. For gemstone setting, choose a steel burnisher with a curved, pointed tip.

Center punch A tool that creates a small dimple in metal when hit with a hammer. The dimple is used as a guide for drilling.

Charcoal block A specially compressed type of charcoal that holds and reflects heat, helping you to solder faster. This block also produces a reducing atmosphere that can help prevent firescale.

Chasing hammer A hammer that's usually used for striking chasing tools, punches, or other hard steel tools such as stamps.

Copper tongs Use instead of steel tongs along with Sparex pickle baths to safely place or remove work; steel tongs can plate the metal jewelry with copper.

Cross-locking tweezers Unlike regular tweezers, locking tweezers stay closed when you let go and open when you squeeze them. Use to get a firm grip on small pieces such as earring posts or jump rings for soldering. Use these along with a third-hand base to position your work and keep your hands free for soldering.

Cross-peen hammer A hammer that has one end that tapers to a chisel-like point (the peen) and a flat face on the other end.

Dapping block and punches A set of tools that is used with a hammer to make domed shapes in metal. Dapping blocks and punches can be made out of wood or steel.

Dividers A device similar to a compass, but without a pencil point, used for scribing lines onto metal.

Fine silver Also known as silver or pure silver. Fine silver is labeled .999, fuses easily, can be soldered, and is very soft.

Firescale The coppery or black oxide that forms on the surface of metals at high temperature. Firescale can be removed by pickle solutions. Often used interchangeably with fire stain to describe oxidation.

Fire stain Fire stain is usually made from copper in the alloy that has been concentrated below the surface by the heat of soldering or annealing. It can be masked by a thin layer of cleaner metal after pickling, but resurfaces during polishing. It causes patterns of discoloration even on polished metal, and can be removed with abrasives.

Flat/half-round bending and forming pliers One jaw of these pliers is flat and the other has a convex curve, making them very useful for bending round shapes such as rings.

Flow point The temperature at which a grade of solder will melt and flow to create a soldered join.

Flush cutters A type of side cutters that leaves a nearly smooth end on trimmed wire. Super-flush and other types of side cutters are also available; follow the manufacturer's rating for the heaviest gauge and type of wire recommended.

Flux A substance applied to metal in the areas to be joined prior to soldering. The heat from the torch creates oxide formations (firescale), which flux helps prevent. More importantly, flux helps solder to flow into seams as it is melted.

French shears A long-handled snip made for cutting metal; the blades are short with narrow points. Other styles of shears are similar, including Euro shears.

Gold-filled To make gold-filled metal, a layer of gold is bonded to a core of less-expensive metal, such as brass or bronze. When exposed, the base metal inside will tarnish and contrast the gold on the outside. The gold layer is thicker than gold plating and can be polished. Often, gold-filled is 1/20th or 5% gold by weight and will be marked with the karat. For example, "GF" or "12k/20" are common stamps for gold-filled jewelry.

Hard soldering High-temperature soldering, commonly used in jewelry on base and precious metals. Hard or jewelry solders flow at temperatures above 1200°F (650°C).

Jeweler's saw A frame that holds a narrow blade with sharp teeth, used to shape metal.

Karat Signifies the relative amount of gold in an alloy; common forms of gold are 10, 12, 14, and 18k (for karat). Pure gold, which is very soft, is marked 24k.

Liver of sulfur A chemical sold in chunk, liquid, or gel form that's used to add a colored patina to metal.

Mallet A hammer with a relatively large head, often made of wood or rawhide. In jewelry making, a rawhide mallet is used to shape metal without marring its surface.

Nonferrous Metals that contain little or no iron. For jewelry purposes, it refers to base and precious metals, such as copper, brass, silver, and gold.

Oxidation Also called firescale and fire stain. During soldering, oxides form on and inside metals such as sterling, copper, brass and alloys of gold, and usually must be removed. See firescale and fire stain.

Pickle An acidic solution that removes flux and oxides from metal after soldering. Pickle solutions range from traditional, caustic chemicals such as Sparex to gentler pickles such as Silver Prep that are nontoxic, citrus-based, and biodegradable.

Planishing Lightly hammering metal to produce a smooth surface finish; also used to increase size.

Ring clamp A tool that holds metal without marring it for filing and other finishing work.

Riveting hammer A hammer with a small head, used in fine work such as making rivets and texturing.

Steel block A small platform of smooth, hardened steel used as a surface for forging metal.

Ring mandrel A cone-shaped rod, usually made of steel, used for forming and sizing rings. Lines on the mandrel correspond to ring sizes.

Soft soldering Soft soldering can also be described as low-temperature soldering. Soft soldering is often done with a soldering iron using solders based on soft metals such as tin. It's used to solder stained glass, electronics, and pipes.

Solder An alloy of metals that melts at a temperature lower than the metals to be joined.

Soldering Joining metals using heat and pieces of solder. Jewelry soldering, the topic of this book, is high-temperature soldering that involves heat of 1325°F (718°C) and above, usually created by a torch.

Solder board A heat-resistant work surface designed for soldering.

Solder pick A pointed steel, tungsten, or titanium rod with a handle used to bring solder to a piece or move parts around while soldering. Titanium picks are best because solder won't melt onto them.

Sweat-soldering A two-step soldering process. First, the solder is melted onto one surface. Then that surface is put in contact with another piece of metal and the solder is drawn to the second surface with heat. Sweat-soldering helps control where solder flows and is the best way to solder two sheets of metal together.

Sterling silver An alloy of 92.5% silver and 7.5% copper. Sterling is also labeled 925. Because of the addition of copper, it is more durable and harder than fine silver, but it tarnishes and develops firescale when soldered.

Texture hammer A hammer with patterns incised on one or both faces, used to add surface texture to metal.

Third hand A heavy base for holding cross-locking tweezers for hands-free soldering.

Tumbler A rotary machine with a barrel that is used to burnish jewelry. Commonly used with stainless steel shot, water, and some burnishing compound or a drop of dish soap for precious-metal finishing.

Tweezers Steel tweezers are used to handle hot pieces of metal and for holding pieces in place during soldering.

Vermeil Gold plating over sterling silver. Gold can be plated over other metals, but to be sold as vermeil in the U.S., the plating must be over sterling.

Sources

Try your local bead shops. They're a great source for stones, beads, wire, and findings. If they offer classes in metalworking, they may also be a good source for tools and supplies. Most hardware stores carry a good selection of sandpaper for metal and some tools that can be used for jewelry making, such as unpolished hammers and cupped nail sets.

Listed below are some online jewelry supply companies that offer excellent products.

Cool Tools
CoolTools.us
888.478.5060

Rio Grande
riogrande.com
800.545.6566

Otto Frei
ottofrei.com
800.772.3456

Thunderbird Supply Company
thunderbirdsupply.com
800.545.7968

111

About the Author

JOE SILVERA earned a B.F.A. degree in metalsmithing with honors and later apprenticed as a goldsmith in southern California. After his apprenticeship, he worked as a model-maker for jewelers in Los Angeles and began selling his own jewelry at fine art galleries and shows across the country.

Joe's favorite technique is carving rings and detailed sculptures of animals for lost-wax casting. Now, with 20-plus years of experience, Joe is a popular metalworking teacher in the San Francisco bay area and across the U.S. His classes and workshops provide a great foundation in the fundamental skills of jewelry making and are mixed with laughter, encouragement, and lots of creativity. Visit his website at silverajewelry.com.

ACKNOWLEDGMENTS

Thank you to my lovely wife, Anat, without whose support and encouragement this book would not be possible. Thank you to all the metalsmiths who shared with me their craft over the years, especially Al Pine and Dieter Muller-Stach. And thank you to my students, who continue to teach me as much as I teach them.